YORK NOTE

General Editors: Professor A
of Stirling) & Professor Suhe
University of Beirut)

Nathaniel Hawthorne

THE
SCARLET
LETTER

Notes by Suzanne Brown

BA (MOUNT HOLYOKE) PH D (DUBLIN)

LONGMAN
YORK PRESS

YORK PRESS
Immeuble Esseily, Place Riad Solh, Beirut.

LONGMAN GROUP UK LIMITED
Burnt Mill,
Harlow, Essex

First published 1981
Second impression 1987

ISBN 0-582-78197-3

Produced by Longman Group (FE) Ltd
Printed in Hong Kong

Contents

Part 1

Introduction

Historical background

Nathaniel Hawthorne (1804–64) was born into a New England which was only a few generations away from the American War for Independence (1775–83). He was one of the earliest writers to see himself as contributing to an American tradition in literature, rather than as working in the English tradition. However, the region of America in which he lived had since the seventeenth century been heavily settled by people from the British Isles, and a radical break with English culture would not have reflected his own experience of American life. He made a real effort to understand the history of New England, spending twelve years after his graduation from Bowdoin, a small liberal arts college in Maine, reading historical records and documents as well as books of more general cultural interest. During this time he also energetically applied himself to writing stories set in New England, and attempted his first novel, *Fanshawe* (1828), which was based partly on his life at Bowdoin College. Another early attempt was a group of stories, 'Seven Tales of My Native Land'. However, neither of these satisfied their author. *Fanshawe* was printed anonymously at his own expense in 1828, but shortly thereafter Hawthorne became so unhappy about its deficiencies that he tried to recall it, and destroyed many copies. He also burnt the manuscript of 'Seven Tales of My Native Land', a gesture which he later made the subject of a short piece called 'The Devil in Manuscript' (1851).

These difficulties were partly caused by the nature of the region whose life he wanted to portray. New England comprised six of the thirteen original English colonies along the Eastern seaboard. Between it and Spanish settlements in the south and south-west lay land mostly still wilderness. Northward was the area now called Canada, where French furtrappers and Indians co-existed. Gradually the French had explored and settled the banks of North America's two great central rivers, the Ohio and the Mississippi. The English settlers had fought against them in a seven year conflict called the French and Indian War (1756-63), during the Anglo-French Seven Years War in Europe. The English settlers' friendly relations with Indians had turned to deep conflict as the two cultures came to be so evidently incompatible. They saw themselves as isolated.

Nor did they feel any close relationship to their mother country England. Rather, as this quotation from John Winthrop's (1588–1644) shipboard sermon (1630) to settlers bound for Massachusetts Bay Colony suggests, the early New Englanders saw themselves in a special bond or covenant with God, redeeming the Old World by making a new society which could act as a leaven in a vast social change. Winthrop told them that their bond 'is by a mutuall consent through a specially overruleing providence, and a more than ordinary approbation of the Churches of Christ to seeke out a place of Cohabitation and Consorteshipp under a due forme of Government both civill and ecclesiasticall'. This covenant was to be taken deadly seriously: 'For wee must Consider that wee shall be as a Citty upon a Hill, the eies of all people are uppon us'.

The society, however, whose earlier generations had seen themselves as fulfilling this religious and social mission, had lapsed into relative apathy over the years. By the third generation Puritan leaders were searching for a way to restore the original fervour. They saw that such fervour was needed to hold their people together during years of hardship. The difficult climate of snowy winters and hot summers, the stony ground, and the rough waters of coastal fishing areas in the Atlantic, made economic survival difficult. Moreover, Europe showed little sign of taking the new society as a moral model. In frustration, the Puritan leaders urged reform and renewal. Religious passion was set alight by blazing rhetoric during the Great Awakening revival sermons preached in New England churches in the early 1740s. Cotton Mather (1663–1728), an eminent Puritan, had recorded real distress at the failure of New England's special mission, in *Magnalia Christi Americana* (1702), but the Great Awakening movement showed that religious zeal was indeed not dead. So too did the earlier tragic witchcraft trials of 1692, in which Hawthorne's ancestor John Hathorne was one of three judges. Indeed New England remained characterised by a strictly Puritan outlook long into the nineteenth century.

However, in Germany and then in England the nineteenth century brought Romanticism, a new set of values quite different from those held by the Puritans. Writers and philosophers of the Romantic Movement emphasised a return to spiritual simplicity and regretted that the new social force of industrialisation was breaking up the older agricultural pattern of village life. They thought of that past as allowing individuals a more natural, more complete mode of expressing their characters in their lives. The Scottish writer Sir Walter Scott (1771–1832) wrote stories about people who lived in earlier times in Scotland. These were enormously popular in the British Isles and in cultivated circles in America. Hawthorne read them with great interest. He also read English Gothic romances, which told of decaying castles, ancestral curses, and lost fortunes, thrilling their wide readership. Hawthorne wanted to be a successful writer of fiction, and more deeply, he was interested in creating for Americans a sense of their past. Thus we can see the New England past was of special interest to Hawthorne for two reasons:

1. He wanted to write distinctively American fiction, not colonial British fiction. Setting his stories in America helped to achieve this aim.
2. As a writer influenced by Romantic thought, he wanted to write about the past. He hoped to adapt some of the techniques of the Gothic romance to the American material.

However, Hawthorne encountered some special difficulties in using historical backgrounds for his romances and short stories:

1. American history was relatively short. He overcame this in different ways in different stories. The events of *The Scarlet Letter* he portrays as being almost unrecorded and almost forgotten in local oral tradition.
2. American colonial history had been dominated by religious quarrelling, which at first glance seemed unpromising material for fiction. Hawthorne tried to turn this weakness to advantage, emphasising the strange, self-enclosing atmosphere of colonial religious traditions.

Biography

Nathaniel Hawthorne was born in Salem, Massachusetts in 1804. His ancestors were a mixture of sane and sensible townsfolk and a more fanatical line of Puritan zealots. Hawthorne wrote in 'The Custom House' (1850) that the earliest American ancestor, William Hathorne 'was present to my boyish imagination as far back as I can remember':

[This man] was a soldier, legislator, judge; he was a ruler in the Church; he had all the Puritanic traits, both good and evil. He was likewise a bitter persecutor, as witness the Quakers, who have remembered him in their histories, and relate an incident of his hard severity towards a woman of their sect, which will last longer, it is to be feared, than any record of his better deeds, although these were many.

One such courageous act was William Hathorne's bold refusal to go with the Massachusetts governor to England in order to explain to Charles II the colony's flouting of royal authority. This man's son John was the Salem judge mentioned earlier, who was one of three involved in condemning witches in 1692. There was a family tradition that one witch had cursed the Hathornes, a belief that appealed to Hawthorne's melancholy imagination. (Nathaniel changed the spelling of the name from Hathorne to Hawthorne after his graduation in 1825.) Hawthorne used this idea of an ancestral curse in his second romance, *The House of the Seven Gables* (1851).

Later generations of Hathornes were simple, law-abiding people, and Nathaniel's own father was a sea captain who died four years after Nathaniel was born. Nathaniel's mother came from a family long involved in business, and her brother Robert was able to give her considerable financial help as she reared her two daughters and her son. Despite these early problems, Hawthorne's own life can be said to have taken an even course through rather stormy times. His sisters nurtured his ambition as a writer, and his mother did not demur when he boasted to her as a boy, 'How proud you would feel to see my works praised as equal to the proudest productions of the scribbling sons of John Bull'. Bowdoin (which he attended from 1821 to 1825) gave him a good education in Classical and Biblical literature, English composition and rhetoric, as well as natural sciences and philosophy. Better still, there he met sympathetic and intelligent friends. The closest of these was Horatio Bridge to whom he wrote twenty-five years later 'If anybody is responsible for my being at this day an author, it is yourself'. Indeed Goodrich, Hawthorne's first publisher, only accepted his first collection of short stories *Twice-Told Tales* (1837) after Bridge had guaranteed him two hundred and fifty dollars if it made a loss. Another college friend was Franklin Pierce, later President of the United States, (who was elected in 1852 and served from 1853 to 1857). When President, he arranged for Hawthorne to become U.S. consul in England, freeing him from financial worry and giving him a chance to see the old world of England and Europe. Longfellow (1807–82), later a distinguished poet, was also at Bowdoin with Hawthorne. He gave the commencement address for their year on the topic 'Our Native Writers':

> Yes – Palms are to be won by our native writers! – by those that have been nursed and brought up with us in the civil and religious freedom of our country. Already has a voice been lifted up in this land, – already a spirit and a love of literature are springing up in the shadows of our free political institutions ... Of the many causes which have hitherto retarded the growth of polite literature in our country ... the greatest which now exists is doubtless the want of that exclusive attention which eminence in any profession so imperiously demands.

A timely encouragement to Hawthorne's literary ambitions came from Longfellow's pen: a very favourable review of Hawthorne's first short-story collection *Twice-Told Tales* (1837) in the respected journal *The North American Review.*

Lucky in his friends, Hawthorne was also lucky in his wife, Sophia Peabody Hawthorne. She combined many accomplishments – she could read Greek, Latin, and Hebrew, studied history, and displayed real ability as an amateur painter and sculptor – with a submissive and gentle nature. She was affectionate, understanding, and helpful to his work. Despite the inevitable difficulties of rearing three children on a modest and uncertain income, Sophia always protected Hawthorne's privacy within the home, giving him a well-furnished study. As a result, Hawthorne could enjoy his growing family without feeling they disturbed his work. Hawthorne had married late; he was thirty-eight when the wedding took place in July 1842. The courtship had been nearly four years long, as Hawthorne had hoped to achieve financial security before marriage, but had finally settled for the small reassurance of a steady income from contributions to periodicals such as *The Democratic Review, The New England Magazine,* and *The Token.* He had briefly held a post in the Custom House at Boston (in 1839 to 1840) and more daringly had ventured a thousand dollars of his savings on the Brook Farm utopian community, joining it in April 1841. There he first worked as a farmhand, and, after five months, lived as a boarder. By November he had become disillusioned about Brook Farm as a possible future home, and felt the effort and the capital were wasted. However, the experience he was later to use in writing *The Blithedale Romance.*

The Hawthornes set up house in The Old Manse, Concord, Massachusetts, which they rented from 1842 to 1845. Hawthorne wrote a light-hearted journal entry about finances in March 1843: 'The Magazine people do not pay their debts so that we taste some of the inconviences of poverty, and the mortification – only temporary, however – of owing money, with empty pockets. It is an annoyance; not a Trouble'. But after the birth of Una, their first child, a year later, his worries about money became more serious.

Again he was fortunate. The political party Hawthorne belonged to, the Democrats, won the Presidential election for their candidate James Polk. Hawthorne's close friend Bridge was now a navy officer, Pierce was a Senator in the upper house of the United States Congress, and he also had O'Sullivan, the editor of *The Democratic Review,* to plead on his behalf for a post. An appointment was offered to him in April 1846 as Surveyor for the District of Salem and Inspector of the Revenue for the Port of Salem. As Salem was not a busy port, this work was not time-consuming, but it paid a real income. Moreover, the boredom of those office mornings Hawthorne turned to good account, when he wrote about them in his piece 'The Custom House' published in 1850 with *The Scarlet Letter.*

Hawthorne had experienced few problems in publishing short stories and essays in periodicals, since his earliest days as a writer. After his first collection *Twice-Told Tales* appeared in book form in 1837 he became widely known, particularly as the pieces had often originally been published anonymously. Other collections followed: *Grandfather's Chair* (1841); a second considerably enlarged edition of *Twice-Told Tales* (1842); *Mosses from an Old Manse* (1846). Throughout the 1840s, Hawthorne's reputation had grown. Intellectuals and fellow-writers such as Orestes Brownson (1842–76), E. A. Duyckinck (1816–78) and Edgar Allan Poe (1809–49) praised his work. Still he had needed to supplement income by editing Bridge's *Journal of an African Cruiser* (1845) and serious reviews of *Mosses from an Old Manse* had not been as favourable as reviews of earlier books. By 1846 Hawthorne himself felt a change of literary direction was needed, but he found himself unable to give much attention to writing while he worked in the Custom House. When the Whig party returned to power in 1848, it ousted many Democrats from posts. Hawthorne was dismissed in June 1849.

The year 1849 was one of crisis for Hawthorne; that summer as he struggled with anger and anxiety over his dismissal, he watched his mother die. Autumn brought renewal; he began a more serious undertaking than he had as yet attempted, his first romance, *The Scarlet Letter*. He worked with total concentration, writing for as much as nine hours a day. Within six months the manuscript was ready for publication. It came out in March 1850, in an edition of two thousand copies, and a second edition ten days later of three thousand copies. With it the publishers Ticknor, Reed, and Fields printed the short autobiographical essay, 'The Custom House'. Hawthorne's original idea had been a collection including *The Scarlet Letter*, 'The Custom House', and other tales, which he thought might be called 'Old Time Legends; together with Sketches, Experimental and Ideal'. He wrote to Fields:

> Is it safe, then, to stake the fate of the book entirely on this one chance? A hunter loads his gun with a bullet and several buckshot; and, following his sagacious example, it was my purpose to conjoin the one long story with half a dozen shorter ones, so that, failing to kill the public outright with my biggest and heaviest lump of lead, I might have other chances with the smaller bits, individually and in the aggregate. However, I am willing to leave these considerations to your judgment, and should not be sorry to have you decide for the separate publication.

Despite Hawthorne's anxiety the book was an immediate success, both with the critics and the reading public. Even the second printing sold well for some months. Critical praise was generous, in both America and England. Hawthorne himself agreed with the objection often made to the story, that it was unrelievedly gloomy. The shadowy atmosphere of his own work often distressed him throughout his life.

A few critics attacked the story as 'immoral' in its sympathy for an unfaithful wife, and a fallen minister. Orestes Brownson, who had liked Hawthorne's earlier work, led the attack in *Brownson's Review*. Hawthorne scorned such remarks, and perhaps noted with some amusement that they only increased sales. Two London publishers brought out pirated editions in the summer of 1850 in which they reprinted the text without permission from either the author or the original publisher. While neither Hawthorne nor his American publisher would receive payment from them, they were both pleased at the popular demand for *The Scarlet Letter* in England.

'The Custom House' caused a local disturbance among Salem people who thought they recognised themselves or their neighbours in Hawthorne's rather comic caricatures. Perhaps it was as well that the loss of political office caused the Hawthornes to move house again, this time to Lenox, Massachusetts, in the Berkshire mountains. The new home was small and simple. It made a retreat for them for a winter and two summers, where Hawthorne found time to delight in his children and in old and new friends. The most lively new friendship was that with Herman Melville (1819–91), whom he met in August 1850. The two writers stimulated each other, speaking, as Hawthorne recorded of one happy occasion, of 'time and eternity, things of this world and of the next, and books, and publishers, and all possible and impossible matters'. Both were hard at work in the winter 1850 to 1851, Melville on *Moby Dick* (1851), Hawthorne on *The House of the Seven Gables*. Each admired the other's work. Melville wrote to Hawthorne of *The House of the Seven Gables*: 'it has robbed us of a day, and made us a present of a whole year of thoughtfulness; it has bred great exhilaration and exultation'. The book came out in April 1851 and was even more successful financially and critically than *The Scarlet Letter*, reaching sales of five thousand within its first year. In the months after its publication Hawthorne wrote a children's book re-telling Classical myths. It was called *The Wonder Book*, and came out in 1852. A satiric piece 'Feathertop' for the *International Magazine* and two prefaces to collections of tales comprised the rest of Hawthorne's output during his stay in the Berkshires.

'Feathertop' was Hawthorne's last short work of fiction, and when *The Snow Image and Other Twice-Told Tales* came out in the 1851–2 winter, it was Hawthorne's last new collection of tales. It contained four pieces written since 1846, when he had published *Mosses from an Old Manse*, along with eleven others of earlier date. Hawthorne's subsequent fiction was more ambitious. After moving again within Massachusetts – this time to West Newton – Hawthorne went to work on *The Blithedale*

Romance. He wrote rapidly, and Ticknor and Fields were printing the book in May 1852.

This was another of Hawthorne's own species of story, the allegorical romance, in which the tale hovers between the world of action and the world of meaning, seeming half in the twilight stillness of a thinking mind. Hawthorne was conscious of writing a new kind of book, and tried to explain his work to his readers. In 'The Custom House' he wrote that he was entering 'a neutral territory, somewhere between the real world and fairy-land, where the Actual and the Imaginary may meet, and each imbue itself with the nature of the other'.

The Blithedale Romance was not as successful as Hawthorne's earlier works, even though Fields had secured its publication in London by the firm of Chapman and Hall. In the spring of 1852 Hawthorne was buying his final Massachusetts home, the Wayside in Concord, so his financial commitments were heavy. His friend Franklin Pierce was running for President, and in June Hawthorne offered to write the campaign biography, feeling not just friendship but a need to involve himself in political life. Pierce won the election the following November. Hawthorne was rewarded with the well-paid post of American consul in England in March 1853. He was delighted, both with the prospect of a good income, and with the chance to see England and perhaps parts of Europe. He was completing a second book of re-told myths for children, *Tanglewood Tales*, which came out that summer. After that, he left himself free to prepare for the voyage to Liverpool. The post lasted the four years of Pierce's presidency and a bit more; Hawthorne found the work very time-consuming and demanding. It involved many public speeches, as well as interviews with Americans in distress, and the entertainment of important visitors. Such a flow of talk left Hawthorne relatively little energy for his own writing. He kept notebooks, however, into which he crowded many impressions of English life. Some of these found their way into his essay collection *Our Old Home* (1863). He attempted to write a romance set in England, to be called 'The Ancestral Footstep', but he had great difficulty with the story, and little spare time to work on it.

After his years of service as consul, Hawthorne took his family to Italy. Sophia had always longed to go there, and found it even more stimulating than she had imagined. The family lived a year there, much of it spent in Rome. If Hawthorne's last major romance, *The Marble Faun* (1860) reflects his own impressions, he found the long Italian past a bit heady and cloying, like a rich meal for one used to frugal fare. The story is really dual; one strand deals with events in the lives of two Italians of distinguished birth, and the other with lives more like those of Hawthorne and his wife, two American artists, who come to love and respect each other. For the Americans in the story, the charm of Italy's heritage of art is marred by her more guilty heritage of abused religion and of demeaning relations between men and women. Their innocence is contrasted with European experience.

The final draft of the story was written in England, as the Hawthornes made their slow progress home. In June 1860 they returned to the Wayside, where Hawthorne was to enjoy the last four years of his life. *The Marble Faun* was selling well on both sides of the Atlantic (in England, under the title *Transformation*). Hawthorne worked on two manuscripts left without final revisions after his death, *Septimus Felton* (1872) and *Dr. Grimshawe's Secret* (1882). He also began 'The Dolliver Romance', and struggled with 'The Ancestral Footstep', but his mind was troubled by the tragic American Civil War (1861–5), especially as his friend Franklin Pierce was widely criticised in the North for having compromised too many principles in trying to prevent it. Hawthorne dedicated his publication *Our Old Home* to Pierce, reaffirming their old friendship and establishing his own moderate political position. He believed that the war should have been prevented, but that since the Northerners had finally undertaken to prevent the Southern States from seceding from the Union and to abolish slavery by force of arms, they must press on for a quick military victory. The victory he saw as acceptable was one that would reclaim only the border States. This was not a popular view.

This stress, and financial and family worries (particularly about the health of his daughter Una) brought Hawthorne to a poor state of health by 1863. He died after a short illness in May 1864. His life with his wife and children left them vivid, happy memories of him. Sophia edited his American, English, and French and Italian notebooks for publication (1868, 1870, 1871), and Rose published *Memories of Hawthorne* in 1897. Una, aided by the noted English poet Robert Browning (1812–89), transcribed *Septimus Felton*, published in 1872, and Hawthorne's son Julian made many contributions to the study of his father's works including an edition of *Dr. Grimshawe's Secret* in 1882, and a two-volume biography, *Nathaniel Hawthorne and His Wife* (1884) and *Hawthorne and His Circle* (1903). In 1876 his publishers brought out a collected edition of Hawthorne's works, and ten other collected editions appeared before 1900, including the standard 1883 twelve-volume edition edited by George Lathrop and published by Houghton Mifflin and Co., Boston.

A note on the text

The Scarlet Letter was first published by Ticknor, Reed and Fields, Boston, 1850. There have been many subsequent reprintings, among them those of the *Complete Works of Nathaniel Hawthorne*, 22 vols., The

Riverside Press, Boston, 1900. This is the autograph edition, in which Volume 6 contains *The Scarlet Letter*.

The Centenary Edition of the *Works of Nathaniel Hawthorne* is being published by the Ohio State University Press, Colombus, Ohio. The first volume was published in 1963; this contains *The Scarlet Letter*. In all, thirteen volumes of this new standard edition have so far been published.

The text used in the preparation of these Notes is that of *The Scarlet Letter* edited with an introduction by Willard Thorpe, Collier Books, New York, 1962, although where there are significant variants, reference is also made to the Everyman Library edition with an introduction by R. W. Butterfield, J. M. Dent & Sons, London, 1906, and last reprinted 1977.

Part 2

Summaries
of THE SCARLET LETTER

A general summary

The Scarlet Letter tells the story of four people whose lives are terribly affected by a community's punishment for adultery. The woman Hester Prynne has been imprisoned and has given birth to a baby daughter before the story opens. Her lover's identity is unknown to her Puritan judges and neighbours in the New England town in which she lives, and she will not disclose his name. When, in Chapter 2, she stands on a pillory scaffold for public ridicule, her husband happens to arrive in the town for the first time. Seeing Hester's shame, he keeps his own identity secret and assumes the name of Chillingworth. He visits Hester in prison, and asks her also to pretend she has never known him. Hester agrees and, when she is released, she and her daughter Pearl go to live on the outskirts of the town alone. Hester supports her daughter and herself with her needlework, the most fantastic example of which is a richly-embroidered scarlet letter A which Hester is compelled to wear always, to show she was an adultress. Her lover never comes forward to console her, and Hester becomes fiercely independent, though she retains a deep love for the man.

Slowly we realise the man is the town's highly respected minister, the Reverend Dimmesdale. As we realise it, so does Chillingworth. He extracts a long, cruel revenge by feigning friendship for the minister, and yet subtly torturing his disturbed conscience. This reaches a crisis one night when the minister stands on the pillory scaffold in the middle of the night, and sees a red A illumine the sky. Hester and Pearl happen to pass by and come to stand with him, a sight seen only by Chillingworth. The minister's health and will to live gradually break down. He has a final secret meeting with Hester in the forest outside the town. She tells him Chillingworth's real identity and purpose, and he and she plan to run away together, back to the old world of England and Europe and away from the Puritan settlements of the New World. However, Hester's little girl does not like the minister and even objects to her mother taking off the embroidered scarlet letter. These omens foreshadow the sad outcome of the story. The minister goes home, and prepares his sermon for the installation of the colony's new governor. When he delivers the sermon Hester and Pearl stand humbly outside the church. After the service, the minister comes out, and climbs up on to the pillory scaffold. He confesses himself to be 'the chief of sinners', and with Hester and Pearl once again beside him he uses his last energy to reveal a scarlet letter in the flesh of his own breast. He collapses and dies in Hester's arms, kissed by Pearl, and free forever of his tormentor. The conclusion of the story relates that Hester and Pearl left the colony, but Hester returned many years later. Chillingworth died soon after the minister, and that man's good fame survived in people's memory despite his confession.

Introductory – The Custom House

This autobiographical essay humorously portrays life in the Salem Custom House while Hawthorne was Surveyor there. It includes satiric descriptions of several of the officials and generally suggests a decaying place of inactivity. Hawthorne paints himself against this backdrop as a dreamy artist whose imagination is strangely stirred by finding a package of documents penned by an earlier Surveyor, and an enclosed embroidery of a large red letter A. One of the documents is a six-page relation of the story of Hester Prynne. Hawthorne then describes himself attempting to turn this material into a romance in the evenings after work. He chides himself for being unsuccessful, but affirms that it was only after losing his post in the Custom House that he found himself able to write. Thus he concludes that his political enemies did him a great service when they turned him out of his job, and that he himself now intends to leave Salem altogether, for the greater benefit of his art.

NOTES AND GLOSSARY:
The pairing of 'The Custom House' with *The Scarlet Letter* has caused much critical comment from Hawthorne's own day to the present. Naturally, some of the earliest critics were the people of Salem who were outraged at this attack on their civic pride. Certainly Hawthorne was venting his private bitterness, as this comment in a letter to Bridge shows:

> As to the Salem people, I really thought that I had been exceedingly good-natured in my treatment of them. They certainly do not deserve good usage at my hands after permitting me to be deliberately lied down – not merely once, but at two several attacks – on two false indictments – with hardly a voice being raised on my behalf; and then sending one of the false witnesses to Congress, others to the Legislature, and choosing another as the mayor.
> I feel an infinite contempt for them – and probably have expressed more of it than I intended – for my preliminary chapter has caused the greatest uproar that has happened here since witch-times. If I escape from town without being tarred and feathered, I shall consider it good

luck. I wish they would tar and feather me; it would be such an entirely novel kind of distinction for a literary man. And, from such judges as my fellow-citizens, I should look upon it as a higher honour than a laurel crown.

However, the essay served other functions for Hawthorne as well as private satisfaction. He hoped to include several pieces in the volume with *The Scarlet Letter*, but his publisher Fields decided to publish only the two works and to do so immediately. Hawthorne was surprised by this decision, because he felt *The Scarlet Letter* was too sombre and serious to sell well without the help of included lighter essays and tales. For financial reasons as well as artistic ones, the newly-ejected Surveyor was anxious for the book to sell well. He even suggested imprinting the title in red on the cover, to help the book to attract notice among the drabber volumes along a bookseller's shelf.

'The Custom House' essay had artistic purpose, too. It helped the reader to move from the humdrum everyday world of common experience to the rich settings and events in Hawthorne's allegorical romance. He wanted to be sure *The Scarlet Letter* would be read with the close attention to the significance of details readers more often give to poems than to works of fiction. He contrasts the nineteenth century daily scene with a half-imaginary past, where all is imbued with an immediate moral significance. In Hawthorne's writing, reflection is not needed to perceive the moral meaning of events, merely apprehension. Ordinary life is quite different, both more commonplace and more confused. By taking a scene of ordinary life as his starting point Hawthorne may have hoped he could more easily persuade his readers that the meaning of the romance was linked to the meaning of their own experience, and that the imaginary past evoked in *The Scarlet Letter* had some message for them from their own community's past.

Hawthorne did find his reading public superficial. He considered them not so much difficult to please as difficult to interest in serious, complicated perceptions. Nineteenth-century Massachusetts's flourishing commercial life, with its risk and enterprise, occupied their imaginations. Politics, including the faction-fighting that would lead to the 1861–5 Civil War, stirred their passions. The older moral passions that had brought their ancestors to America, seemed to be dying into a fireside twilight glow of rectitude, of God blessing their prosperity. Hawthorne's deep belief that the past was still a lively influence in the present was challenged by this. To interest the readers in the serious aspect of *The Scarlet Letter* Hawthorne needed to impart his own sense that the religious missionary zeal of their stern forebears was continued even in their own less vital pursuits, and should be remembered and understood.

He needed to convince them that the price paid for success in their community, as well as in Hester's, was often too high. In both communities people sacrifice their own natural development to accommodate themselves to the available roles, but in Hester's theocratic Puritan town religious passion gave an additional force to the social pressure, and people perhaps stunted or warped themselves believing they thus made themselves fit not just for New England but for heaven. In a grotesque contrast, the sleepy, silly, or base fellow-workers at the Salem Custom House destroy themselves to no purpose beyond comfort or money. They live out their lives without any religious awakening: 'These men – seated, like Matthew, at the receipt of customs, but not very liable to be summoned thence, like him, for apostolic errands – were Custom House officers'. If early Salem was tinder-dry, ready to explode in its terrible witchcraft trials of 1692, the Salem Hawthorne lived in was emotionally chilly and damp.

In 'The Custom House' sketch Hawthorne describes, perhaps fictitiously, his personal rediscovery of the past through the documents and the red letter:

> While thus perplexed, – and cogitating, among other hypotheses, whether the letter might not have been one of those decorations which the white men used to contrive, in order to take the eyes of Indians, – I happened to place it on my breast. It seemed to me, – the reader may smile, but must not doubt my word, – it seemed to me, then, that I experienced a sensation not altogether physical, yet almost so, as of burning heat; and as if the letter were not of red cloth, but red-hot iron. I shuddered, and involuntarily let it fall upon the floor.

In locating the story in the historical past of New England, Hawthorne is saying that the story is especially significant for his American readers. It is their culture's beginnings that he is examining. The introduction gives him a chance to emphasise this claim to their attention. By playing with the idea of ghostly voices speaking to him as he thinks about the story, he is telling readers that the past will reach out to them, will grip them, as a ghostly hand might, and that the voice with which the ghost addresses them, will have something familiar about it. The introduction argues what the story will also take as theme: that a sense of the past is as natural to the imagination as the sense of taste is to the body. It can be dulled or destroyed only at the individual's peril, for it belongs to him and is part of what he needs to live. That past will not always be pleasant, or easy to live with, it may even endanger present happiness. But it has its legitimate claim to make, and like the ghostly voices that address the would-be author, will make itself heard.

autobiography: memoirs of one's life written by oneself
decorous: proper and seemly

prolix:	wordy and long-winded
truculency:	fierceness
tarpaulins:	canvas, waterproofed with tar, used for covering hatches, ships' boats, here slang for sailors
emoluments:	profits from office, including salary
vicissitude:	change of fortune
eulogium:	praise
cumbrous:	burdensome
esoteric:	understandable only to the initiated few
inditing:	composing
anatto:	a yellow-red dyestuff from the Caribbean
dearth:	scarcity
chirography:	skilled handwriting

Detailed summaries

Chapter 1: The Prison-Door

In Chapter 1 a crowd is gathered at the prison-house door. They are gloomy people, taking a sad relish in the occasion that has brought them together, the public punishment of a young woman for adultery. Hawthorne describes the prison building, which is dark, gloomy, and ugly. He tells us it is surrounded by weeds, except for one wild rose-bush in bloom as the story opens.

NOTES AND GLOSSARY:
In Chapter 1 Hawthorne is already using physical details to indicate some more abstract meaning: he tells us the rose-bush may have sprung up under the footstep of 'the sainted Ann Hutchinson' who was imprisoned for her religious beliefs. He says, 'it may serve, let us hope, to symbolise some sweet moral blossom that may be found along the track, or relieve the darkening close of a tale of human frailty and sorrow'.

In this last sentence Hawthorne is establishing the predominant emotion, or *tone*, of the story. It is sad, but something in the moral lives of some characters will enliven that sorrow and give it a purpose.

It is worth noticing that the opening chapter has not introduced the main characters. Rather, it has been used to set the scene for them. They enter in Chapters 2 and 3.

Isaac Johnson:	Isaac Johnson died in 1630, the same year as his arrival with the first Boston settlers. His land provided the site for the prison, graveyard, and church
inauspicious:	unlucky
portal:	doorway

Ann Hutchinson: she lived from 1591 to 1643, and preached a rejection of 'salvation by works' and a belief in the intuitive revelation of God's indwelling 'grace'

Chapter 2: The Market-Place

When Chapter 2 opens the women gathered at the prison door are talking among themselves. All but one feel the adultress is not being punished harshly enough. The most severe wishes her to be condemned to death. Only one young wife says that the punishment, always to wear a scarlet letter A on the breast of her gown, must be very humiliating: 'not a stitch in that embroidered letter, but she has felt it in her heart'. Hester is led out of prison by the beadle; she carries her infant daughter. On her gown she has embroidered the punishing letter A 'with an elaborate embroidery and fantastic flourishes of gold thread'. The Puritan colonies required people to dress in sombre colours, so Hester's gown is the only one in town gaudily decorated. Hawthorne tells us that her dress 'seemed to express the attitude of her spirit, the desperate recklessness of her mood, by its wild and picturesque peculiarity'. The beadle leads her to stand on the pillory scaffold, where by custom wrongdoers were frequently condemned to stand in public view, for public abuse, sometimes with hands and head locked into a wooden frame called the stocks. Hester is not in the stocks; she retains a natural dignity as she stands on the raised platform.

NOTES AND GLOSSARY:
In Chapter 2 Hawthorne speaks directly to us, criticising any use of the stocks. Later he remarks that a Papist would have thought Hester looked like the Madonna, Jesus's mother, as she suffered her punishment. He thus reminds readers that the story is set in a time and place different from our own and in a different culture that we must try to understand. He suggests that he himself does not share the values of the society he is writing about. Hawthorne will intrude into the story in this way from time to time, although more often the story will simply proceed without his commenting upon it. Certainly Hawthorne will not always reveal his attitude when the reader might expect him to; however, he will make it plain that he is not in full agreement with the views of any of his main characters. This is one way in which Hawthorne's writing can seem 'ambivalent', as many critics have termed it. Ambivalence means the author's exact attitude seems unsettled.

Hawthorne allows the reader to know what Hester is thinking as she stands holding her baby on the scaffold of the pillory. She endures the solemn stares of the crowd and of the officials of Church and State as best she can. She vividly remembers scenes from her childhood and girlhood in England. She thinks of her parents who were part of the hereditary aristocracy in England, but who had little money. She remembers her husband as he then seemed to her:

> ... a pale, thin, scholar-like visage, with eyes dim and bleared by the lamplight that had served them to pore over many ponderous books. Yet those same bleared optics had a strange, penetrating power, when it was their owner's purpose to read the human soul. This figure of the study and the cloister, as Hester Prynne's womanly fancy failed not to recall, was slightly deformed, with the left shoulder a trifle higher than the right.

She recollects going with him to 'a Continental city' (later we learn this was Amsterdam, a Protestant city in the Netherlands where many English Puritans resettled after leaving England). However, her present suffering breaks through all these memories:

> She turned her eyes downward at the scarlet letter, and even touched it with her finger, to assure herself that the infant and the shame were real. Yes! – these were her realities, – all else had vanished!

physiognomies:	faces, as revealing of characters
bond-servant:	one bound to service without wages
Antinomian:	one who holds that, under the gospel dispensation, the moral law is of no use or obligation, faith alone being necessary to salvation
Quaker:	one of a religious sect founded by George Fox (1624–91), about 1650, the members of which call themselves *Friends*. The name *Quaker* was applied in derision in 1650 by a judge to Fox, who bade the justice tremble at the word of the Lord
town-beadle:	a minor parish official, one of whose duties was to lead processions
sumptuary:	relating to or regulating expenditure
meridian:	noonday
Papist:	a Roman Catholic, considered as a partisan of the Pope

Chapter 3: The Recognition

Chapter 3 introduces Chillingworth, Hester's wronged husband. He is recognised by no one but Hester, who says nothing. Neither does she reveal her lover's name, when pressed to do so by the clergy. The distinguished Reverend Wilson then preaches to the crowd on the sin of adultery, dwelling on the horrors of sin and of the punishment of sin so that the crowd comes to regard Hester almost with superstitious awe.

NOTES AND GLOSSARY:

When we are introduced to Chillingworth he has come to the edge of the crowd, in the company of an Indian. He seems himself to be 'clad in a strange disarray of civilized and savage costume'. Hawthorne tells us two contradictory things about his physical appearance, that 'there was a remarkable intelligence in his features, as of a person who had so cultivated his mental part that it could not fail to mould the physical to itself, and become manifest by unmistakable tokens' and that 'his face darkened with some powerful emotion, which, nevertheless, he so instantaneously controlled by an effort of his will, that, save at a single moment, its expression might have passed for calmness'. This indicates a central feature of this character: he is disguised, secretive. It seems natural that the first gesture we see of his in the story is his silent admonition to Hester to keep his identity secret: 'When he found the eyes of Hester Prynne fastened on his own, and saw that she appeared to recognize him, he slowly and calmly raised his finger, made a gesture with it in the air, and laid it on his lips.' The painful relationship between these two characters does not really change throughout the rest of the story. It is always characterised by secrecy and unhappiness.

It is matched by Hester's other relationship with a man, also secret and unhappy. As Hester stands publicly for punishment, this man too will not acknowledge his bond with her. He will not admit he is the father of her child. She keeps his identity secret just as she does her husband's. Though Hester has known two men, she and the baby are completely alone as the crowd watches them.

Hester is asked to identify her lover by the distinguished eldest clergyman of Boston, John Wilson. He is physically above Hester, as well as socially and morally, but Hawthorne speaks directly again, to criticise him: 'He looked like the darkly engraved portraits which we see prefixed to old volumes of sermons; and had no more right than one of those portraits would have to step forth, as he now did, and meddle with a question of human guilt, passion, and anguish'.

His questioning does not bring a response and so he asks the local minister Dimmesdale to urge Hester to reveal her lover's name. Hawthorne then introduces the third main character; the reader sees him first as the crowd sees him:

The directness of this appeal drew the eyes of the whole crowd upon the Reverend Mr. Dimmesdale; a young clergyman, who had come from one of the great English universities, bringing all the learning of the age into our wild forest land. His eloquence and religious fervour had already given the earnest of high eminence in his profession. He was a person of very striking aspect, with a white, lofty, and impending brow, large, brown, melancholy eyes, and a mouth which, unless when he forcibly compressed it, was apt to be tremulous, expressing both nervous sensibility and a vast power of self-restraint. Notwithstanding his high native gifts and scholar-like attainments, there was an air about this young minister, – an apprehensive, a startled, a half-frightened look, – as of a being who felt himself quite astray and at a loss in the pathway of human existence, and could only be at ease in some seclusion of his own. Therefore, so far as his duties would permit, he trod in the shadowy by-paths, and thus kept himself simple and childlike; coming forth, when occasion was, with a freshness, and fragrance, and dewy purity of thought, which, as many people said, affected them like the speech of an angel.

He too speaks from the balcony but he speaks movingly of what the reader will later understand is Dimmesdale's situation: 'Be not silent from any mistaken pity and tenderness for him; for, believe me, Hester, though he were to step down from a high place, and stand there beside thee, on thy pedestal of shame, yet better were it so, than to hide a guilty heart through life'. He also points to what will be revealed as his own weaknesses, hypocrisy and moral cowardice. The baby lifts up her arms to him, but Hester will not tell her lover's name. Dimmesdale puts his hand on his heart, as he says 'Wondrous strength and generosity of a woman's heart! She will not speak!'. This gesture is repeated many times in the course of the story; it suggests hiding real emotions.

The main characters have now all adopted their first resolutions; Hester chooses dignity in isolation, Chillingworth a secretive revenge, and Dimmesdale a furtive remorse. Against their private dramas is the reaction of the crowd – like a chorus in a Greek tragedy, they comment at every crucial phase. They listen to a sermon by the Reverend Wilson on sin and are moved to regard Hester with horror. Hawthorne speaks sensitively of Hester's suffering without magnifying it. In this way he keeps her before his reader's imagination as a real woman, and not just as a symbolic, suffering scapegoat.

visage:	face
heterogeneous:	having unlike kinds mixed
abate:	lessen
ignominious:	dishonourable and humiliating
Richard Bellingham:	Bellingham (1592–1672) was governor of the Massachusetts colony in 1641, 1654, and 1665–72
halberds:	long-handled weapons especially in use in the fifteenth and sixteenth centuries
John Wilson	Wilson (*c.*1591–1667) was an English Congregational minister who came to Boston with the first settlers
sagacity:	wisdom

behoves:	to be necessary for, especially as a duty or obligation
exhort:	advise or warn earnestly

Chapter 4: The Interview

Hawthorne uses Chapter 4 to clarify the new relationship between Hester and Chillingworth. Hester and the baby are distressed after their ordeal; Chillingworth is sent for, as a physician. He uses the chance to speak privately to Hester, demanding her lover's name. She will not tell him, but he avows he will discover it for himself, and take a private revenge.

NOTES AND GLOSSARY:

In this chapter, Hester begins in simple fear of her husband, but ends in greater fear and defiance. The medicine he prepares for herself and the baby she fears may be poisoned. When she has drunk it safely they enter into conversation. Chillingworth admits she never loved him and freely says 'we have wronged each other'. He adds:

> Mine was the first wrong, when I betrayed thy budding youth into a false and unnatural relation with my decay. Therefore, as a man who has not thought and philosophized in vain, I seek no vengeance, plot no evil against thee.

However, he wants to revenge himself on her lover, and asks her his name. She refuses to tell him; 'That thou shalt never know'. He replies 'with a smile of dark and self-relying intelligence. "Never know him! Believe me, Hester, there are few things, – whether in the outward world, or, to a certain depth, in the invisible sphere of thought – few things hidden from the man who devotes himself earnestly and unreservedly to the solution of a mystery"'. Hester responds with Dimmesdale's own gesture of clasping her hands over her heart. Chillingworth promises that he will neither harm nor denounce her lover once he has found him out, but adds: 'Let him hide himself in outward honour, if he may! Not the less he shall be mine!'. Hester senses this secret revenge as terrible. She shudders too when Chillingworth asks her to swear to keep his identity secret, but she does as he asks. Throughout the story, Hester recognises the social code as a fact she must face, a burden she must bear, even though she does not agree with it; so when her husband asks her for this oath, she obeys his wishes. By their marriage he has become someone with power over her, but Hester fears him and even compares him to the devil, the personification of tempting evil. 'Art thou like the Black Man that haunts the forest round about us? Hast thou enticed me into a bond that will prove the ruin of my soul?' His strange reply suggests that he is almost pleased by the comparison: '"Not thy soul," he answered, with another smile. "No, not thine!"'.

Chillingworth is the first character in the story to become allegorised. The reader has watched him dedicate his life to revenge. This sole purpose has used his energy to the exclusion of other purposes, and has thus reduced his personality to one emotion, schemed for and relished. Instead of seeming to have the simplicity that a figure in an allegory or fairy tale has from the outset, this dark-minded alchemist has become a black magician before the reader's eyes. Hawthorne describes this psychological process so quickly or deftly in two chapters that it is necessary to stop and reflect that he has revealed not a bad person, but a strange person, becoming bad.

Indian sagamores:	lesser tribal chieftains
amenable:	yielding
trundle-bed:	a low bed that may be pushed under another bed
alchemy:	medieval chemical science
simples:	medicinal plants
Lethe:	in Greek mythology, a river of the underworld whose water when drunk causes the dead to forget all life
Nepenthe:	a potion or drug used by the ancients to drown all pain or sorrow
Paracelsus:	a Swiss alchemist and doctor (1493–1541)
balefire:	the fire of the funeral pyre

Chapter 5: Hester at Her Needle

This chapter relates the gradual changes in Hester's state of mind after she is released from prison. It bridges the time between the first scenes and later events in the story, a period of about three years.

NOTES AND GLOSSARY:
The process by which a character becomes allegorised interests Hawthorne very much. Earlier he had shown Chillingworth turning to one evil purpose; now, writing of Hester's suffering, he treats of her transformation. Throughout 'the accumulating days, and added years' Hester 'giving up her individuality' becomes

> the general symbol at which the preacher and moralist might point, and in which they might vivify and embody their images of woman's frailty and sinful passion. Thus the young and pure would be taught to look at her, with the scarlet letter flaming on her breast, – at her, the child of honourable parents, – at her, the mother of a babe, that

would hereafter be a woman, – at her, who had once been innocent, – as the figure, the body, the reality of sin. And over her grave, the infamy that she must carry thither would be her only monument.

Hawthorne himself treats her more subtly, pointing out that she is complicit in her suffering; she could have left New England and taken up a new life elsewhere. The psychological process by which Hester comes to accept her limited role and live within it, fascinates Hawthorne. He tries to describe it:

> But there is a fatality, a feeling so irresistible and inevitable that it has the force of doom, which almost invariably compels human beings to linger around and haunt, ghostlike, the spot where some great and marked event has given the color to their lifetime; and still the more irresistibly, the darker the tinge that saddens it.

He adds, 'there dwelt, there trode the feet of one with whom she deemed herself connected in a union', an idea that comes to Hester almost as a sinful temptation. Finally he sums up:

> What she compelled herself to believe – what, finally, she reasoned upon, as her motive for continuing a resident of New England – was half a truth, and half a self-delusion. Here, she said to herself, had been the scene of her guilt, and here should be the scene of her earthly punishment; and so, perchance, the torture of her daily shame would at length purge her soul, and work out another purity than that which she had lost; more saintlike, because the result of martyrdom.

Hester moves to a small thatched cottage remote from the town. She lives there with her baby daughter, and the place itself becomes allegorised in the minds of the townspeople: 'A mystic shadow of suspicion immediately attached itself to the spot'.

But her ordinary life must continue, so Hester earns money by sewing. Her beautiful handiwork is not used for the pleasure of men and women in fine clothes. Fine clothes are not normally approved of by this grim society. Hester is only allowed to sew beautiful embroidery for babies, for the dead, and for men of power. Her art cannot choose its subjects, but must serve the chosen symbols of her society. Daily she must serve the society which rejects her, in the way it chooses. In a final sad note, Hawthorne tells the reader that she was never asked to embroider a bridal veil. 'The exception indicated the ever-relentless vigour with which society frowned upon her sin'. Hester's only rebellion is the beautiful clothing she makes for her daughter Pearl. Joy in needlework she rejects, like all other joys, as sin. Hawthorne speaks sharply about this: 'This morbid meddling of conscience with an immaterial matter betokened, it is to be feared, no genuine and steadfast penitence, but something doubtful, something that might be deeply wrong, beneath'. Later he adds: 'she was patient, – a martyr, indeed, – but she forebore to pray for enemies; lest, in spite of her forgiving aspirations, the words of the blessing should stubbornly twist themselves into a curse'. He shows how her social banishment warps her nature, and she grows to have a dread of children and of strangers. Her imagination is 'somewhat affected' and she comes to feel that she can see the hidden sins of others. Hawthorne neither affirms nor denies that she is able to do this. He merely remarks that such loss of faith is one of the saddest results of sin, and leaves his readers to wonder whether Hester sees truly.

He concludes the chapter with a fantastic touch. The vulgar, he says, come to have a legend that the scarlet letter is red-hot, and glows in the dark. As so often in the story, Hawthorne comes close to the border-country of allegory and fairy-tale. However, he twists the image into a psychological analogy: 'And we must needs say, it seared Hester's bosom so deeply, that perhaps there was more truth in the rumour than our modern incredulity may be inclined to admit'.

inscrutable:	incapable of being fully known or understood
retribution:	repayment
plebeian order:	lower classes
insidious:	wily and sly
contumaciously:	in a manner which suggests resistance to authority

Chapter 6: Pearl

Chapter 6 introduces Hester's child Pearl. Hawthorne tells of her strange development into a mischievous, solitary child whose impulsive outbursts of strong feeling puzzle and sometimes distress her mother.

NOTES AND GLOSSARY:
Some critics consider Pearl an important character in the story; others do not. Pearl does not make a choice about how to live, as the other central characters do. She simply reacts to her situation emotionally and mentally. She is graceful and beautiful, lively and imaginative, but her bold and reckless acts trouble her mother. Hawthorne seems to agree with Hester's perception:

In giving her existence, a great law had been broken; and the result was a being whose elements were perhaps beautiful and brilliant, but all in disorder; or with an order peculiar to themselves, amidst which the point of variety and arrangement was difficult or impossible to be discovered. Hester could only account for the child's character – and even then most vaguely and imperfectly – by recalling what she herself had been during that momentous period while Pearl was imbibing her soul from the spiritual world, and her bodily frame from its material of earth. The mother's impassioned state had been the medium through which were transmitted to the unborn infant the rays of its moral life; and, however white and clear originally, they had taken the deep stains of crimson and gold, the fiery lustre, the black shadow, and the untempered light of the intervening substance.

Hester sometimes wonders if Pearl is not wilder than any human child, as if she were partly a mischievous spirit. She does not seem to return her mother's love with any simple tenderness, but only with an occasional moody passion of affection. Pearl is made stranger by being a social outcast among the other children. Several times in the chapter Hawthorne speaks of her being like a little witch, or an imp, or an elf. He tells of her strange imaginative games, playing that weeds and trees are the Puritan children and their parents, who must be killed if she is to be safe. Pearl seems fiercely to train herself to struggle in a hostile world.

She is fascinated by the scarlet letter Hester wears. One day she plays a target game, throwing wild flowers at it and jumping up to dance when she hits it. Hester is driven to ask, 'Art thou my child, in very truth?'. Pearl says, 'Yes; I am little Pearl'. Hester plays with her and asks, 'Tell me, then, what thou art, and who sent thee hither'. Pearl becomes serious and asks 'Tell me, mother!'. But to Hester's reply 'Thy heavenly Father sent thee!', Pearl defiantly cries 'I have no heavenly Father!'. Hester grieves over this, remembering that some townspeople whisper the idea that Pearl has a demon father. This superstition Hawthorne does not support, but neither does he scorn it. Pearl is, to Hester, a living person whose nature reflects her mother's sin and unquiet heart. So, a third time, the reader can watch a character allegorised by other characters and, partly, by herself. Even her name suggests the allegory; she is Hester's 'pearl of great price', like that spoken of by Jesus in Matthew's gospel (Matt 13:45–6) when He tells of a merchant who sells all that he has to get one pearl and then says that the 'kingdom of heaven' is such a pearl.

This description of Pearl has brought the story along a few years in time so that events of a later date can now be related. In later events Pearl will continue to reflect her mother's state of mind in her moods, although in other ways she is ungovernable by Hester, or indeed by anyone else.

imbibing:	taking in
caprice:	wilful sudden impulse
anathemas:	curses
phantasmagoric:	like a rapid and shifting succession of things seen or imagined, as in high fever, delirium

the dragon's teeth: in a Greek myth, Cadmus sows the teeth of a dragon he has slain, and they sprout up fighting men, who kill one another until only five are left

Luther: Martin Luther (1483–1546), father of the German Reformation, who preached the priesthood of all believers, and salvation by faith alone, not by good works

Chapter 7: The Governor's Hall

Chapter 7 takes place when Pearl is three. It describes the little journey of Hester and Pearl, going to Governor Bellingham's mansion to deliver embroidered gloves.

NOTES AND GLOSSARY:

Chapter 7 is the prelude to an encounter of all the main characters, Hester, Dimmesdale, Chillingworth, and Pearl. They will meet when Hester delivers embroidered gloves to Governor Bellingham. Hester wants to use the occasion to confront Governor Bellingham about his plan to take Pearl away from her, for others to rear. Pearl has come with her, wearing a beautifully embroidered red tunic that reminds everyone who sees it of Hester's scarlet letter. On their way to the Governor's mansion, Pearl is taunted by Puritan children, as 'the likeness of the scarlet letter'. She rushes fiercely at them and they run away. Unafraid, she continues the trip with her mother. The Governor's house is cheerful and liberally decorated outside with broken glass embedded in stucco, and with 'seemingly cabalistic figures and diagrams' drawn into the stucco while it was wet. Pearl wants to play with the sunlight that flashes off the glass, but Hester sadly says, 'No, my little Pearl! Thou must gather thine own sunshine. I have none to give thee!'.

They are admitted by an indentured servant, someone virtually owned by the master for seven years, although originally free-born. This strikes a foreboding note. The interior of the house is designed and fitted as a grand English home might be, although the portraits of severe, unsmiling men strike a second foreboding note. Pearl delights in a shining new suit of armour hung on one wall. In its curved surfaces the scarlet letter reflects monstrously, seeming almost to hide Hester behind itself. This is a third foreboding note.

Hester then persuades Pearl to view the Governor's garden. It too looks as if it were modelled on an English style, but 'The proprietor appeared already to have relinquished, as hopeless, the effort to perpetuate on this side of the Atlantic, in a hard soil and amid the close struggle for subsistence, the native English taste for ornamental gardening'.

There are a few rose-bushes and Pearl cries out for a red rose. This reminds us of the rose-bush at the prison door in Chapter 1 and of the red roses of much passionate love poetry. The Governor enters with Reverend Wilson, Reverend Dimmesdale, and Dr Chillingworth as the chapter closes.

ludicrous: ridiculous
pristine: primitive and uncorrupted
***Chronicles of England*:** Richard Holinshed's *Chronicles of England, Scotland, and Ireland* (1577), a popular historical compilation used by Shakespeare as a source-book for his plays
cuirass: breastplate of a suit of armour
gorget: a piece of armour protecting the throat
greaves: armour-pieces for the legs below the knees
gauntlets: armour gloves, or gloves to protect the hands
Pequod War: a war in 1637 against the Pequot Indians of Connecticut, in which the tribe was crushed
Francis Bacon: Bacon (1561–1626), a Lord Chancellor of England, was deeply interested in the new scientific method
Sir Edmund Coke: Coke (1552–1634) was Lord Chief Justice, a defender of the common law, and famous parliamentarian and jurist. He wrote the classic *Reports and Institutes* (1628–44)
William Noye: Noye (1577–1634) was Attorney General and author of legal commentaries
Sir John Finch: Finch (1584–1660), Baron of Fordwich, was, at various times, King's Counsel, Speaker of the House of Commons, and Chief Justice
eldritch: weird and eerie

Chapter 8: The Elf-Child and the Minister

Chapter 8 describes the meeting of Hester, Dimmesdale, Chillingworth, and Pearl, in the presence of Governor Bellingham and Reverend Wilson. Pearl's future is hotly debated, and only Dimmesdale's defence prevents Hester losing the child.

NOTES AND GLOSSARY:

Both Governor Bellingham and the Reverend Wilson are described as easygoing men who enjoy worldly and sensuous pleasure, even though they are very stern to public sinners like Hester. The other two men are much more unusual. Hawthorne repeats without comment the popular view that Chillingworth is Dimmesdale's friend and doctor, helping him as his health fails under the strain of many good works.

The Governor first espies Pearl and compares her to the children of the Lord of Misrule in Christmas masques at the English Court of King James I. (He ruled from 1603–25). Masques were a highly stylised form of drama in which actors wore masks. Like her mother, the Reverend Wilson asks her who she is, and if she is an elf-child. 'I am mother's child, and my name is Pearl!' she bravely responds. They notice Hester then, and the Reverend Wilson mentions that they have been discussing Hester and Pearl.

The Reverend Wilson asks Pearl who made her, but the naughty child does not give the answer Hester has taught her. Instead she says she has not been made at all, but plucked by her mother off the bush of wild roses that grew by the prison door. The Governor is horrified, and wants to settle the matter at once, but Hester grabs her child. 'God gave me the child' she cries.

> He gave her, in requital of all things else which ye had taken from me. She is my happiness! – she is my torture, none the less. . . . See ye not, she is the scarlet letter, only capable of being loved, and so endowed with a millionfold the power of retribution for my sin?

She appeals to the minister who comes forward, his hand over his heart as it was in the first scene at the pillory. He looks deeply troubled but defends her right. 'God gave her the child, and gave her, too, an instinctive knowledge of its nature and requirements, – both seemingly so peculiar, – which no other mortal being can possess. And moreover, is there not a quality of awful sacredness in the relation between this mother and this child?'.

He eloquently persuades them to allow Pearl to stay with her mother, though the Governor grudgingly insists that Pearl be examined in religious matters by a minister from time to time, and be sent both to school and to church when she is older.

Pearl shows a strange sympathy for the minister. She places her hands on his and rests her cheek against his hand, in a gesture of trust and tenderness. Dimmesdale looks around and hesitates before returning the gesture with a kiss of his own, but Pearl rejects such timid and tentative love. She laughs and runs away. The Reverend Wilson says she has witchcraft in her, a frightening remark to make even half-seriously in a society which would try and hang witches.

Roger Chillingworth, whom Hester has shuddered to see looking uglier and 'duskier' than when they last met, says 'Would it be beyond a philosopher's research, think ye, gentlemen, to analyse that child's nature, and, from its make and mould, to give a shrewd guess at the father?', but the Reverend Wilson puts him off: 'Nay; it would be sinful, in such a question, to follow the clue of profane philosophy'.

In conclusion, Hawthorne relates an incident that 'it is averred' happened as Hester leaves with Pearl. He does not tell us who claims it happened or whether he takes it to be true, for it belongs to the shadowy region of human feeling on which he makes no definitive comment. Mistress Hibbins, Governor Bellingham's sister who was later executed as a witch calls to Hester, 'Wilt thou go with us tonight? There will be a merry company in the forest; and I well nigh promised the Black Man that comely Hester Prynne should make one'. Hester smilingly replies, 'I must tarry at home, and keep watch over my little Pearl. Had they taken her from me, I would willingly have gone with thee into the forest, and signed my name in the Black Man's book too, and that with my own blood!'.

expatiating: enlarging in discourse or writing

scarlet woman: this, and 'woman of Babylon' are terms of abuse used by Reformers to refer to the Roman Catholic Church; from the Book of Revelation in the Bible

New England Primer: an alphabet primer (*c.*1683) which used verses and woodcuts on Biblical themes

Westminster Catechism: a book teaching by question and answer the theology of John Calvin (1509–64) formulated by the Westminster Confession (1645–7) for the English churches, principally Presbyterian and Congregational, but also some Puritan. There were 'shorter' and 'longer' Westminster catechisms

depravity: total sinfulness. Calvin thought that the total depravity of man's soul contrasted with the absolute holiness of God

indefeasible: incapable of being made null and void

mountebank: a charlatan in a travelling show

tithing-men: parish officials responsible for maintaining order

baggage: a common term for a woman of low repute

Chapter 9: The Leech

Chapter 9 picks up the thread of Chillingworth's story, and connects it to Dimmesdale's. It relates the manner in which the two men come to know each other, and describes the relationship which develops.

NOTES AND GLOSSARY:

Hawthorne reminds the reader of Chillingworth's chosen isolation:

Unknown to all but Hester Prynne, and possessing the lock and key of her silence, he chose to withdraw his name from the roll of mankind, and, as regarded his former ties and interest, to vanish out of life as completely as if he indeed lay at the bottom of the ocean, whither rumor had long ago consigned him.

After that choice, his unnatural life continues: 'This purpose once effected, new interests would immediately spring up, and likewise a new purpose; dark, it is true, if not guilty, but of force enough to engage the full strength of his faculties'. These plans he conceals by posing as a doctor, taking up residence in the town. The chapter title, 'The Leech', refers to his work as a doctor, or leech, and also to his unnatural life – drawing strength from the sufferings of others, as the leech lives by sucking blood from its victims. Chillingworth gradually attaches himself to the Reverend Dimmesdale in such a way that he slowly drains the minister of life. The elder ministers of Boston and the deacons of his own church have both urgently recommended the minister to the doctor's care, but under that care the minister slowly worsens, despite a seeming friendship that develops. The two men spend much time together. Eventually they rent rooms in the same house.

The public has always seen the young minister as directly involved in the struggle between good and evil. The congregation sees in Dimmesdale a special messenger from God summoning them to holy work, but now they also see him as being ravaged by some personal struggle. As they watch his health fade despite Chillingworth's concern and care, they change their view of Chillingworth. Instead of being a heaven-sent healer, he becomes a suspect alchemist, whose distillations are fuelled by infernal fire. Hawthorne partly defends their new perception: 'When an uninstructed multitude attempts to see with its eyes, it is exceedingly apt to be deceived. When, however, it forms its judgment, as it usually does, on the intuitions of its great and warm heart, the conclusions thus attained are often so profound and so unerring, as to possess the character of truths supernaturally revealed'. But while using the common view to describe the deterioration of Chillingworth's character, and his hold over the minister, Hawthorne reveals a more intimate truth to his readers. Many people believe Chillingworth to be Satan or Satan's emissary, haunting the young minister who struggles in agony towards triumph, but 'Alas! to judge from the gloom and terror in the depths of the poor minister's eyes, the battle was a sore one, and the victory anything but secure'.

appellation:	name
chirurgical:	surgical
Elixir of Life:	an alchemic term for a substance for prolonging life indefinitely
pharmacopoeia:	a book describing drugs, chemicals, and other medicinal preparations
Sir Kenhelm Digby:	Digby (1603–65) was an adventurer and writer who discovered that oxygen is necessary to plant life
Gobelin looms:	the looms of a famous Parisian family, the Gobelins, who wove precious tapestries

David and Bathsheba: a story from the Bible, II Samuel 11–12. King
David sends a soldier Uriah to certain death in
battle in order to wed his wife Bathsheba, but God
sends Nathan the prophet to condemn the king

Sir Thomas Overbury's murder: Overbury (1581–1613), a writer, was
poisoned by the connivance of the lewd Countess of
Essex, after he opposed his patron's marriage to
her. Dr Forman (1552–1611) was an astrologer and
seller of love potions who was implicated in her
affairs

Chapter 10: The Leech and His Patient

In this chapter Chillingworth closes in on his prey, Dimmesdale. In the
final paragraphs, while Dimmesdale sleeps the doctor opens his
patient's shirt and sees something which throws him into a wild delight.

NOTES AND GLOSSARY:
This chapter delves more deeply into the disturbing relationship
between Chillingworth and Dimmesdale. On the surface the two men
seem to be living together in harmonious friendship. They are both
lonely intellectuals, with every reason to be glad of intelligent
companionship. Moreover, the younger man seems to need the doctor's
care that Chillingworth eagerly supplies. However, below the surface,
the emotional reality is quite different from what it seems. Hawthorne
describes Chillingworth as a miner digging into the soil of the other
man's personality, throwing away real gold while he searches for
something without value. Dimmesdale does not voluntarily help him.
He resists Chillingworth's prying as best he can, but as time goes on his
health fades and he is weakened. The frequent close contact between
them gives Chillingworth repeated chances to probe and pry. One
conversation between them ends stormily, with Dimmesdale saying 'But
who art thou, that meddlest in this matter? – that dares thrust himself
between the sufferer and his God?'. Even this interview leaves
Chillingworth curious: 'As with one passion, so with another! He hath
done a wild thing ere now, this pious Master Dimmesdale, in the hot
passion of his heart!'. Dimmesdale, because of his depression, trusts no
one as a true friend and does not recognise his enemy. The brief sight of
Hester and Pearl through the window merely underlines his isolation. In
his loneliness, he soon apologises for his outburst and he and
Chillingworth continue to live in the same house, meeting often.
Chillingworth is now certain Dimmesdale's ill health comes from a bad
conscience, by 'a strange sympathy betwixt soul and body'. The wicked
physician finds out what he wants to know at last. The minister has

fallen asleep in a chair, and Chillingworth opens his shirt, without waking him. Hawthorne does not reveal what he sees, but whatever it is

> Had a man seen old Roger Chillingworth, at that moment of his ecstasy, he would have had no need to ask how Satan comports himself when a precious human soul is lost to heaven, and won into his kingdom.

The reader is left to guess that it may be a scarlet letter.

Bunyan:	John Bunyan (1628–88) wrote of hell's gates flaming across the pathway of the pilgrim Christian, in his famous allegorical work *The Pilgrim's Progress* (1678)
proximity:	nearness
that day:	Judgement Day, on which Puritans believed all souls would reveal all their secrets and thus show forth the justice and the mercy of God
importunate:	troublesomely urgent
palliate:	mitigate

Chapter 11: The Interior of a Heart

In this chapter Hawthorne chronicles Dimmesdale's decline into near-madness, as he is tormented with malicious skill by Chillingworth.

NOTES AND GLOSSARY:

This chapter describes how Chillingworth uses his new knowledge. Rather than exposing the minister to public shame he pretends he knows nothing and continues in the same friendly way as before, but he is able to torment Dimmesdale slyly. Dimmesdale cannot understand why he is coming to hate and fear Chillingworth. Because of piety, Dimmesdale will not allow himself to break off the seeming friendship. His self-discipline has its own kind of courage, which is reflected in the vigour and vision with which he preaches.

Dimmesdale finds his secret an increasing burden. He tries to relieve his feelings by telling his congregation that he is a vile sinner, but he does not name his sin. Puritan rhetoric often embellished a sermon by speaking of the awful gulf between the holiest of men and the holy God; Dimmesdale's apparent confessions are taken for such phrases. He himself knows this, and gets no relief from his anguish. However, because he suffers, he truly stirs his congregation to moral awakening. He both comforts and challenges them. Dimmesdale knows this, too, and it makes real confession seem almost selfish.

He punishes himself privately, by fasts, vigils, and scourging, but these acts only weaken him further. He has hallucinations, including a repeated one of Hester leading Pearl and pointing first at her scarlet letter and then at himself. So it is revealed for certain that Dimmesdale is Hester's guilty partner in adultery.

To the minister, symbolic hallucinations have become almost more real than the ordinary physical world, and symbolic action has become a need. As the chapter closes, he steals out of the house one dark night, fully dressed.

preternatural: beyond the normal
abstruse: profound and difficult to comprehend
Pentecost: in the Bible, Acts 2:1–11, the Holy Spirit descends upon Jesus's apostles and closest disciples enabling them to preach, being understood by each listener in his own language
Enoch: Enoch 'walked with God' and 'was translated', without dying, to Heaven according to the Bible, Genesis 5:21–4 and Hebrews 11:5

Chapter 12: The Minister's Vigil

The minister goes to the pillory scaffold and stands there in shame. He laughs hysterically and is noticed by Hester and Pearl who come to stand with him. Pearl asks him to stand with her in daylight, but he refuses. A red A flashes across the sky, and in its light, Pearl sees Chillingworth. He comes forward and leads the distracted minister home. The next day many people report seeing the A and a sexton tells Dimmesdale his glove has been found on the scaffold. Dimmesdale preaches with great power, but does not confess.

NOTES AND GLOSSARY:
The minister goes to the pillory scaffold where Hester had endured her public humiliation. He stands upon it, unseen by anyone 'save that ever-wakeful one which had seen him in his closet, wielding the bloody scourge'. He shrieks aloud but the town sleeps on. Only Governor Bellingham and his sister the witchlike Mistress Hibbins look out from their windows. A bit later the Reverend Wilson passes by the scaffold, going home from the deathbed of Governor Winthrop. He carries a lantern but he does not see Dimmesdale, and Dimmesdale does not speak to him. After a time, the minister imagines the town awakening, and finding him still on the scaffold. He laughs hysterically, and the laugh seems echoed by a child's laugh. He calls out to Pearl and Hester, coming from measuring Governor Winthrop's body for a shroud. He asks them to come up and stand with him. Silently they do. He feels their vital strength uphold him.

Pearl asks the crucial question, 'Wilt thou stand here with mother and me, tomorrow noontide?'. 'Nay; not so, my little Pearl. ... Not so, my child. I shall, indeed, stand with they mother and thee, one other day, but not tomorrow'. Pearl presses him again with her question and he tells her he will stand with them on the Final Day of Judgement which the Puritans believed would happen after the End of the World. Pearl laughs at this admission. She is a creature of this world.

A meteor flashes across the night sky. To the minister it seems to streak a red letter A across the night sky. In this scene Hawthorne comes close to describing events as supernatural. He is at pains to tell his readers that there is a tradition of portents in the sky foreshadowing events that affect the life of the New England community, but it is not clear whether by referring to this he is expressing belief in portents, or accounting for Dimmesdale's belief that he saw the red A. If a reader believes that this latter is Hawthorne's intention, the chapter's end will surprise him, for in it the old sexton tells Dimmesdale next morning that many people saw a red A in the sky, which they interpret to stand for Angel, heaven's sign that the soul of Governor Winthrop is now with God.

The meteor illumines the street and Pearl mischievously points out Roger Chillingworth watching them. The minister recognises him with horror. He asks, 'Who is that man, Hester? ... I shiver at him! Dost thou know the man? I hate him, Hester!'. Hester's oath to Chillingworth keeps her silent. It is Pearl who offers to tell him more of Chillingworth. When he bends to her, she whispers nonsense into his ear. The minister asks her 'Dost thou mock me now?', and Pearl responds 'Thou wast not bold! – thou wast not true!'.

Chillingworth comes forward, pretending it is only a night-madness of Dimmesdale's to be out with Hester and Pearl on the scaffold. He offers to lead the minister home, and Dimmesdale weakly goes. The next day Dimmesdale's divided self is made even more evident. He preaches a sermon of great power, but when the sexton offers him his glove, found upon the scaffold, he allows the man to be mystified at how it got there, even to believe it a trick of Satan. When the sexton tells him of the portent in the sky, he compounds his silence with a lie, 'I had not heard of it'.

Geneva cloak: black cloak commonly worn then by Calvinist ministers recalling by its name John Calvin's association with Geneva

John Winthrop: trained in law, Winthrop (1588–1649) was a founder of the Massachusetts Bay Colony in 1630, and was almost continuously re-elected Governor or deputy Governor until his death

defunt transgressor: dead sinner

gable peaks:	the vertical-triangle roof characteristic of a certain style of New England colonial buildings
straitly:	carefully
sexton:	an under-officer in a church among whose duties are care of church property, bell-ringing, and in some cases, grave-digging
scurrilous:	indecent and abusive

Chapter 13: Another View of Hester

Chapter 13 recounts the changes in Hester's personality and outlook over the years of solitude. It describes her strange relationship with her community, to whom she is an accepted figure, welcome in time of trouble or sickness, but not an accepted person, whose own concerns might be shared by them.

NOTES AND GLOSSARY:
This chapter explores the changes in Hester's life and personality after seven years of social isolation. Her meeting with Dimmesdale has re-awakened in her soul a sense of their bond. Hawthorne subtly remarks:

> The links that united her to the rest of humankind – links of flowers, or silk, or gold, or whatever the material – had all been broken. Here was the iron link of mutual crime, which neither he nor she could break. Like all other ties, it brought along with it its obligations.

Their relationship, and her duty toward Pearl, are the only active roles she has found, but her very passivity, meekly letting society make her an outcast, has slowly brought her into a degree of public affection. This allows her to enter houses where someone is sick or dying as a nurse and helper. She is excluded from the ordinary flow of life, but included in times of crisis. Some people say that her letter A no longer stands for adultress, but for Able, because they recognise her great emotional strength.

Hawthorne does not see the change in Hester's character as enobling. He says her womanly tenderness is crushed deep into her heart. Her life has become dominated by thought, leaving little freedom for affections. While the Puritan community is coming to admire Hester – believing even that a heathen Indian's arrow miraculously struck her breast and fell away without injuring her – Hawthorne sees her as a natural woman leading a stunted life. Moreover he shrewdly recognises two effects this has on her personality. Firstly, mental freedom being the last private freedom left to her, she will use it eagerly in wide-ranging speculation. Secondly, her repressed passions are imprisoned and not tamed. Their energy remains youthful and unspent. Their force remains narrowly channelled. So when Hester discerns that Dimmesdale is truly threatened by Chillingworth, she has both the freedom of mind and the energy of character to tackle the doctor herself.

gibe:	sarcastic and taunting words
tribunal:	court
wreak:	to give free course to

Chapter 14: Hester and the Physician

Chapter 14 describes Hester's confrontation with Chillingworth, her attempt to get him to treat Dimmesdale in a kinder way.

NOTES AND GLOSSARY:
Hester meets Chillingworth one day out walking; she is shocked by his change in character. 'In a word, old Roger Chillingworth was a striking evidence of man's faculty of transforming himself into a devil, if he will only, for a reasonable space of time, undertake a devil's office'. Before her, Chillingworth glories in his revenge.

'Yea, woman, thou sayest truly!' cried old Roger Chillingworth, letting the lurid fire of his heart blaze out before her eyes. 'Better he had died at once! Never did mortal suffer what this man has suffered. And all, all in the sight of his worst enemy! He has been conscious of me. He has felt an influence dwelling always upon him like a curse. He knew, by some spiritual sense, – for the Creator never made another being so sensitive as this, – he knew that no friendly hand was pulling at his heart-strings, and that an eye was looking curiously into him, which sought only evil, and found it. But he knew not that the eye and hand were mine! With the superstition common to his brotherhood, he fancied himself given over to a fiend, to be tortured with frightful dreams, and desperate thoughts, the sting of remorse, and despair of pardon; as a foretaste of what awaits him beyond the grave. But it was the constant shadow of my presence! – the closest propinquity of the man whom he had most vilely wronged, and who had grown to exist only by this perpetual poison of the direst revenge! Yea, indeed, he did not err, there was a fiend at his elbow! A mortal man, with once a human heart, has become a fiend for his especial torment!'

Here, as in many other passages, Hawthorne mixes the natural with the supernatural. Chillingworth is like a fiend or devil, although he is truly a man. This description of Chillingworth is similar to the earlier description of Hester as the 'self-ordained Sister of Mercy' whom arrows could not hurt, in that it mixes the natural with the supernatural. However, it differs, in that this is Chillingworth's view of himself, and not the ordinary townsfolk's view. Hester's view of herself is also coloured by faith in the supernatural. She tells Chillingworth that if she no longer deserved to wear the stigmatising letter A it would drop off of its own accord. Chillingworth sneers at this, telling her to wear it if she will, but about himself he is deterministic and almost superstitious. He sees it as his fate to become a man of evil. He refers her to the dark view of God's power that some Puritans held, that God knew in advance some people were damned but created them anyway for damnation. Hester has moved far away from these views. She intends to try to rescue Dimmesdale from his sufferings. She will not believe that she, Dimmesdale, or even Chillingworth are necessarily damned. She asks Chillingworth to take the initiative and forgive Dimmesdale, thereby freeing himself as well from the deadly power of sin. When he refuses, she still intends to do what she can for Dimmesdale.

The chapter shows the relationship between Chillingworth and Hester altering: after Hester tells Dimmesdale who Chillingworth really is, their marriage will no longer be a secret bond between them. Hester is moving into the world of action. From now on she will not be simply a victim enduring punishment for past action, but an active person once again. Hester has always cared for Pearl and taken responsibility for her, but from now on, she will also take responsibility for Dimmesdale, and perhaps even for herself.

propinquity: nearness
peradventure: if by chance

Chapter 15: Hester and Pearl

Chapter 15 shows how these changes in Hester's outlook affect her relationship with her daughter Pearl, as Pearl grows a little older.

NOTES AND GLOSSARY:
Pearl, at seven, is still a wild and free child, untamed by the ordinary experiences of play with other children. She lives in a private world of mischievous fantasy; her heart has only the beginnings of tenderness, not any real and developed feeling. Hester has loved her intensely, and seen her nature in the best possible light, but still somewhat mistrusts whether Pearl returns her love.

Hawthorne describes the games Pearl plays as Hester converses with Chillingworth. She plays with her own reflection in a pool; she makes shell-boats and torments a couple of tiny sea animals. She throws stones at gulls; she dresses as a mermaid, decorating herself with a green letter A made of eel-grass. There is a strand of cruelty in Pearl's play, but there is also vitality and imagination. She is unregenerate, that is, a natural child who makes no moral effort. However, in this chapter, Hawthorne shows the first glimmer of Pearl's moral and social intelligence that

Hester has ever seen. Pearl comes when her mother calls, and speaks with her mother about the scarlet letter. Hester's question, 'Dost thou know, child, wherefore thy mother wears this letter?' brings a clever response: '"Truly do I!" answered Pearl, looking brightly into her mother's face. "It is for the same reason that the minister keeps his hand over his heart!"'. However when Hester presses her about what she knows she responds curiously: 'But in good earnest now, mother dear, what does this scarlet letter mean? – and why doest thou wear it on thy bosom? – and why does the minister keep his hand over his heart?'. Hester realises this is the beginning of a more serious investigation of life by her quixotic little girl but she avoids answering because she wishes to protect Dimmesdale. Hawthorne has suggested that it is possible for Pearl to develop a moral nature, but has not yet shown her fulfilling that possibility. The reader must wait to see if she will do so. Hawthorne also reveals that Hester may hinder Pearl's development although she loves Pearl deeply. Hester's forbidden love for Dimmesdale continues to create problems for herself and Pearl. She cannot stop herself from hating Chillingworth or from lying to her daughter. Hawthorne allows the reader to see that these shortcomings trouble Hester, but he leaves it unclear whether he himself considers her blameworthy. He makes it plain in this chapter that simple repentance of adultery is not possible for Hester. She loves Dimmesdale not just with her body but with her spirit, and destroying love would be a greater sin than adultery. To do it she would have to annihilate her own personality.

verdure:	green vegetation
sedulous:	diligent
deleterious:	hurtful
deadly nightshade, dogwood, and henbane:	deadly nightshade and henbane produce poisons possessing magical powers according to ancient folklore and necromancy; together with dogwood they are in the pharmacopoeia of witchcraft
horseshoe:	horseshoe crab
five-fingers:	starfish
hornbook:	a tablet used to teach spelling. Early ones usually consisted of a cover of transparent horn and a single sheet of parchment bearing the alphabet and perhaps a prayer
precocity:	tendency to exceptionally early development
asperity:	harshness

Chapter 16: A Forest Walk

In this chapter Hester does tell Pearl something of the real meaning of
the scarlet letter, as they walk together in the forest. In the distance they
see Dimmesdale. Hester asks Pearl to wait for her, while she goes to him
for a private conversation.

NOTES AND GLOSSARY:

Hester wants to meet Dimmesdale to warn him of Chillingworth's real
identity and malicious intentions. She wants to encounter him outside,
away from everyone except, of course, Pearl, who must go wherever her
mother goes. She enters a forest that has never been settled, and to her
mind it seems like 'the moral wilderness in which she had so long been
wandering'. As she feels anew the wildness of her own nature, she
notices again the wild beauty of Pearl's nature. She and Pearl speak
again about the scarlet letter.

'Mother,' said little Pearl, 'the sunshine does not love you. It runs
away and hides itself, because it is afraid of something on your bosom.
Now see! There it is, playing a good way off. Stand you here, and let
me run and catch it. I am but a child. It will not flee from me – for I
wear nothing on my bosom yet!'

'Nor ever will, my child, I hope,' said Hester.

'And why not, mother?' asked Pearl, stopping short, just at the
beginning of her race. 'Will not it come of its own accord when I am a
woman grown?'

'Run away, child,' answered her mother, 'and catch the sunshine! It
will soon be gone.'

The sunlight does seem to disappear as Hester approaches though
Pearl's face remains bright. Hawthorne says Pearl needs a grief 'to
humanise her and make her capable of sympathy'. He shows how,
without it, she may become cruel. She teases Hester with questions
about the Black Man. Her moral imagination is awakening, but her fate
is partly dependent upon Hester's guidance. This time Hester takes her
daughter's need seriously.

'But, mother, tell me now! Is there such a Black Man? And didst thou
ever meet him? And is this his mark?'

'Wilt thou let me be at peace, if I once tell thee?' asked her mother.

'Yes, if thou tellest me all,' answered Pearl.

'Once in my life I met the Black Man!' said her mother. 'This scarlet
letter is his mark!'

Gradually Hawthorne builds up an impression of the forest as a special
place, a symbolic landscape. The serious conversation between Hester

and Pearl can take place here where the secluded, dense forest allows them a real privacy. Another serious conversation will happen here that could happen in no other place. Hester will meet again with Dimmesdale. Hester tries to create privacy for them, by asking Pearl to go off and play. Pearl agrees, but not until she has seen who approaches and has asked pointedly about the minister's habit of holding his hand over his heart. 'Is it because, when the minister wrote his name in the book, the Black Man set his mark in that place? But why does he not wear it outside his bosom, as thou dost, mother?' Hester will not answer this but her reply suggests that she may eventually tell Pearl what she wants and needs to know: 'Go now, child, and thou shalt tease me as thou wilt another time'. Increasingly, Hester's attention shifts away from the past to the future. Slowly the characters are changing, and a crisis begins to loom in the affair that most concerns them all.

ulterior:	further
Apostle Eliot:	John Eliot (1604–90) was a Cambridge graduate who emigrated to America in 1631 and was the first to preach to the Indians in their own dialects
primeval:	belonging to the first ages and since then, undisturbed
scrofula:	a tuberculous condition most common in children
loquacity:	talkativeness

Chapter 17: The Pastor and His Parishioner

In Chapter 17 Hester meets Dimmesdale and they speak freely about their lives. They resolve to run away, with Pearl.

NOTES AND GLOSSARY:
This crucial chapter reveals for the first time the intensity of the lovers' deep bond. They are alone and in intimate conversation. It is a scene of great passion, felt all the more deeply because of the long denial of passion. Hester does not call the minister by his title, but by his full name. He returns this acknowledgement of mutual love and knowledge, but his nervous vigour has so failed him that he must ask if she is a ghost. She is so struck by this that she also asks him 'dost thou yet live?'. The forest is now completely defined, as a place where souls encounter each other without social constraint or hindrance.

So strangely did they meet, in the dim wood, that it was like the first encounter, in the world beyond the grave of two spirits who had been intimately connected in their former life, but now stood coldly shuddering in mutual dread, as not yet familiar with their state, nor wonted to the companionship of disembodied beings. Each a ghost, and awe-stricken at the other ghost. They were awe-stricken likewise at themselves, because the crisis flung back to them their consciousness, and revealed to each heart its history and experience, as life never does, except at such breathless epochs. The soul beheld its features in the mirror of the passing moment. It was with fear, and tremulously, and, as it were, by a slow, reluctant necessity, that Arthur Dimmesdale put forth his hand, chill as death, and touched the chill hand of Hester Prynne. The grasp, cold as it was, took away what was dreariest in the interview. They now felt themselves, at least, inhabitants of the same sphere.

Without a word more spoken, – neither he nor she assuming the guidance, but with an unexpressed consent, – they glided back into the shadow of the woods, whence Hester had emerged, and sat down on the heap of moss where she and Pearl had before been sitting.

The minister can ask Hester the question that love prompts: 'Hester, . . . has thou found peace?'. He can trust her love to tell her of his suffering. He can also tell her that, like herself, he is not able to repent. 'Of penance, I have had enough. Of penitence, there has been none!' However, he lacks her vital energy. He needs to see his true nature reflected in the knowledge others have of him if he is going to continue living.

Had I one friend – or were it my worst enemy! – to whom, when sickened with the praises of all other men, I could daily betake myself, and be known as the vilest of all sinners, methinks my soul might keep itself alive thereby. Even thus much of truth would save me! But now, it is all falsehood! – all emptiness! – all death!

Hester tells him

'Such a friend as thou hast even now wished for,' said she, 'with whom to weep over thy sin, thou hast in me, the partner of it!' – Again she hesitated, but brought out the words with an effort. – 'Thou hast long had such an enemy, and dwellest with him, under the same roof!'

In reacting with violent emotion, the minister shows that his passions, like Hester's, are repressed rather than disciplined and refined. At first his anger is directed at Hester, but when she begs forgiveness for keeping Chillingworth's real identity secret, the minister's wrath becomes directed toward the false physician. 'That old man's revenge has been blacker than my sin. He has violated, in cold blood, the sanctity of a human heart. Thou and I, Hester, never did so!' The anger mixes with bleak despair and self-loathing. In weakness, Dimmesdale lingers with Hester in the forest. They agree to run away together, back across the ocean over which they had separately come many years before. To

Hester, this pledge is the vindication of her own love, and the values she truly holds. To the minister, it is flight from disgrace.

contiguity: proximity
misanthropy: hatred of mankind
satiating: satisfying to the point of glutting

Chapter 18: A Flood of Sunshine

Dimmesdale and Hester enjoy a brief time of happiness together. However, when they attempt to include Pearl, she does not wish to join them.

NOTES AND GLOSSARY:
This chapter is an interlude of happiness for the troubled pair. However, as they enjoy each other's company and speak freely, the reader becomes aware of the wide gap the years have made between their sensibilities. Hester has become independent in her mind. She has lived estranged from the social system in which Dimmesdale is a great figure. She cannot accept its authority. Dimmesdale feels that the only worth of his life has been his service to that church and state. He has made no private world in which he can live with dignity. She throws aside her cap and scarlet letter. She wants to leave 'these iron men' and re-enter the tolerant, more worldly culture of Europe. Dimmesdale's work has been to call people to dedicate their best efforts to this new theocratic society. If he leaves for Europe he is admitting total defeat. Briefly he feels a wild joy in his decision to do so, and his natural personal vitality seems to return. He responds eagerly when Hester urges him to speak to Pearl, his daughter.

But Pearl represents the distance between Hester and the minister as well as their bond. She has grown for seven years knowing one parent intimately and the other not at all. She has no reason to trust Dimmesdale's proffered love. Nor does she feel the respect for a minister any other child of the town would feel. Hawthorne reminds us how wild her solitary childhood has made her; he portrays her playing with the animals, and eating wild fruit.

A wolf, it is said, – but here the tale has surely lapsed into the improbable, – came up, and smelt of Pearl's robe, and offered his savage head to be patted by her hand. The truth seems to be, however, that the mother-forest, and these wild things which it nourished, all recognize a kindred wildness in the human child.

She decorates herself with violets, anemones, columbines, and twigs. She belongs to the forest, where her parents are taking an afternoon's relief from the prying eyes of townsfolk. When she hears her mother's voice she comes only slowly, because she sees Dimmesdale.

colloquy:	a somewhat formal conference
expiating:	atoning for
nymph-child:	in Greek and Roman mythology a nymph was a lesser goddess of nature, represented as a beautiful maiden living in a forest, meadow, or stream
dryad:	a wood nymph supposed to inhabit trees

Chapter 19: The Child at the Brook-Side

Hester summons Pearl, but the child will not come until her mother again wears the scarlet letter. Even then, she will not accept Dimmesdale.

NOTES AND GLOSSARY:

This chapter foreshadows the final crisis of the book. As Dimmesdale and Hester wait eagerly for Pearl, she refuses to come to them. Hester is upset and almost angry; Dimmesdale just becomes more and more agitated. First he tells Hester that children do not usually like him, but as he becomes more upset by Pearl's little tantrum, he begs Hester to find some way to pacify their daughter.

Hester realises that it is the change in her appearance which is antagonising Pearl. The child misses the scarlet letter and the severe white cap which usually conceals her mother's beautiful dark hair. More deeply, Pearl misses her usual sense that she is the only person her mother loves. Moreover, Pearl has mixed feelings about the minister. He senses this, to the extent that when she stares at him, he covers his heart with his hand.

Hester takes up the scarlet letter again and pins it on to her dress. She puts on her cap. The change in her appearance is 'withering', like 'a gray shadow' falling over her, but Pearl is pleased and runs to kiss her. 'Now thou art my mother indeed! And I am thy little Pearl!' The strange little girl then kisses the scarlet letter and asks chillingly, 'Why doth the minister sit yonder?' Hester speaks of his yearning love for them, but Pearl is sceptical. 'Doth he love us? . . . Will he go back with us, hand and hand, we three together, into the town?' Hester must say no, but speaks of a future when they will share a home. Again Pearl asks a barbed question: 'And will he always keep his hand over his heart?'. She will not willingly come to him. When he kisses her, she runs to the brook and washes his kiss away. Then she sits apart, while Hester and Dimmesdale make their plans.

hieroglyphic:	a character in the picture-writing of the ancient Egyptians and Mexicans
gesticulating:	gesturing
grimaces:	making wry faces

Chapter 20: The Minister in a Maze

This chapter reveals the minister's new state of mind after his interview with Hester. He still has divided loyalties.

NOTES AND GLOSSARY:

Chapter 20 follows Dimmesdale through the rest of that day and night. His mind and feelings are in complete upheaval. The hypocrisy which has eaten away at him has also been his strength, giving him the impetus to do all his public tasks meticulously. Even as he plans to desert his public role and run away with Hester and Pearl to Europe he finds himself planning to give his Election Sermon. This is to be given on the day the new Governor of Massachusetts assumes office; it is a major local public occasion. However, the minister's newly awakened private feelings run against that state of fervour which would prepare him for preaching, and he is in great turbulence of mind. Hawthorne describes how he is assailed by temptations he had never before experienced, and his frail strength nearly gives way to madness. Yet he continues to sense a renewed physical vigour. With great psychological insight, Hawthorne points out that the thought of rebelling against Puritan New England and deserting it, causes the minister suddenly to see its strict pieties as ridiculous. He longs to whisper blasphemies to an aged church deacon, or an argument against individual immortality to a good old woman. He feels the great power he has over the minds of others through his ministry. It is all he can do to refrain from planting a seed of evil in the mind of a young girl who greets him. His better self, along with his harshly trained intellect and religious feeling, is thrown into confusion. He wonders, 'Am I mad? or am I given over utterly to the fiend?'. Mistress Hibbins, 'the reputed witch lady' who had earlier approached Hester, now speaks to him: 'So, Reverend Sir, you have made a visit into the forest'. When he denies it, she laughs:

> 'Well, well, we must needs talk thus in the daytime! You carry it off like an old hand! But at midnight, and in the forest, we shall have other talk together!'

When at last he reaches his study, he feels himself such a different person that it is almost as if he is entering someone else's room, someone he half pities and scorns. Yet, at a knock, he is afraid an evil spirit may enter his room. When Chillingworth comes in, the reader wonders if in some sense that *is* what happens.

Chillingworth easily perceives that the minister now knows he is a deadly enemy, but they both keep up a studied politeness. Chillingworth urges the minister to work on his sermon, as with his failing health, he may not live long. Dimmesdale pretends to agree. Once Chillingworth is gone, the minister sends for food, which he eats hungrily. Then he throws his sermon on the fire and begins another draft. He writes until sunrise, carried on by a great wave of released emotion. The dam has burst, but the flood waters are running into both old and new channels.

irrefragable:	undeniable
obeisance:	deference or homage
buckramed:	stiffened

Chapter 21: The New England Holiday

The action of this chapter takes place on the day of the Governor's installation. Hester and Pearl are in the crowd. There they meet the sea captain whom Hester hopes will take them and Dimmesdale back to the Old World. He tells her Chillingworth has also booked a passage.

NOTES AND GLOSSARY:

This chapter, describing Hester and Pearl in the crowd waiting for the new Governor's procession, is a parallel to the opening chapter of the book, when the crowd waited for Hester to come out of prison to stand with Pearl on the pillory scaffold. However, today Hester moves quietly in the crowd; public attention will be on the newly-installed Governor and the minister. The general mood is merry and festive. Pearl, already disturbed by Hester's repressed excitement, becomes more perturbed by the unusual liveliness of the townsfolk. She asks Hester about Dimmesdale and Hester replies: 'He will be there, child, . . . but he will not greet thee today; nor must thou greet him'. Pearl cannot understand this.

> In the dark night-time he calls us to him, and holds thy hand and mine, as when we stood with him on the scaffold yonder! And in the deep forest, where only the old trees can hear, and the strip of sky see it, he talks with thee, sitting on a heap of moss! And he kisses my forehead, too, so that the little brook would hardly wash it off! But here, in the sunny day, and among all the people, he knows us not; nor must we know him! A strange, sad man is he, with his hand always over his heart!

Into the town come sailors, who are generally allowed to speak more freely and dress more gaily than the local population. It is as if the Puritans recognise that outside their community different standards are observed. No one even remarks on it when the ship's captain speaks to Hester. Yet at the same time, the beadle is stopping a broadsword exhibition-fight on the town's scaffold, lest it violate the serious tone of the day.

The news that the sea captain imparts to Hester startles and upsets her: Chillingworth has also booked a passage on board his ship. Hester looks away, only to catch a glimpse of the evil doctor, smiling menacingly at her.

metropolis: the mother city of a colony
Lord Mayor's show: held on November 9 each year, it marked the inauguration of the Lord Mayor of London with a festival, including a procession
jocularity: jesting
arraigned: called at the bar of a court to answer an indictment
depredations: despoilings
animadversion: adverse criticism

Chapter 22: The Procession

Chapter 22 vividly highlights the contrast between the minister's life and Hester's. She stands outside the church as he begins his Election Sermon inside.

NOTES AND GLOSSARY:
Before Hester can consider what to do about the captain's news, the formal procession with its military escort starts to the strains of military music. The real pride of place, however, is enjoyed by the men of civic importance, the magistrates and the minister. Seeing him fully involved in the glory, power, and seriousness of his office, Hester realises he will give herself and Pearl no glance of recognition. She feels almost hopeless. Pearl too comprehends his withdrawal from them. She asks if it is the same minister who kissed her by the brook. Hester can only answer, 'We must not always talk in the market-place of what happens to us in the forest'. But Pearl persists:

> I could not be sure that it was he; so strange he looked . . . . Else I would have run to him, and bid him kiss me now, before all the people, even as he did yonder among the dark old trees. What would the minister have said, mother? Would he have clapped his hand over his heart, and scowled on me, and bid me be gone?

Pearl is not the only one to embarrass Hester. The old witch-woman Mistress Hibbins garrulously expresses amazement at the minister looking so spiritually vital:

> When the Black Man sees one of his own servants, signed and sealed, so shy of owning to the bond as is the Reverend Mr Dimmesdale, he hath a way of ordering matters so that the mark shall be disclosed in open daylight to the eyes of all the world! What is it that the minister seeks to hide, with his hand always over his heart? Ha, Hester Prynne?

Then Pearl wants to know what Mistress Hibbins means, and in the reply Hawthorne lets us see how close Pearl is to becoming an apprentice of witchery.

> Thou thyself wilt see it, one time or another. They say, child, thou art of the lineage of the Prince of the Air! Wilt thou ride with me, some fine night, to see thy father? Then thou shalt know wherefore the minister keeps his hand over his heart!

As Hester stands outside, the minister has begun to deliver his sermon inside the meeting house. Hester does not attempt to enter, but she can hear every word. To Hester and to his congregation, there seems to be an undertone of real anguish in his powerful speech. Everyone's emotions are deeply affected, as the sermon goes on relentlessly.

Pearl scrambles away from her mother. She runs first to an Indian and then to a mariner. They are not part of the congregation; they can enjoy her play. The sea captain who had spoken to Hester gives her a gold chain to deck herself with, and a message. She is to tell Hester that the doctor plans to bring Dimmesdale aboard with him. He calls her 'witch-baby' and she replies in kind: 'Mistress Hibbins says my father is the Prince of the Air! . . . If thou callest me that ill name, I shall tell him of thee, and he will chase they ship with a tempest!'

Hester hears this news sadly, feeling that there really is no escape for herself and Dimmesdale. As if to emphasise this, a rude crowd of country people come close to Hester staring at the scarlet letter. They leave a space around her. Again, as so often before, she senses both her solitude and her captivity. Some of the townsfolk also stare at her idly, intensifying her suffering. Inside the meeting house, the minister reaches the peak of his power, outside Hester knows only rejection. Hawthorne makes a dramatic contrast:

> While Hester stood in that magic circle of ignominy, where the cunning cruelty of her sentence seemed to have fixed her forever, the admirable preacher was looking down from the sacred pulpit upon an audience whose very inmost spirits had yielded to his control. The sainted minister in the church! The woman of the scarlet letter in the market-place! What imagination would have been irreverent enough to surmise that the same scorching stigma was on them both!

compliance:	act of yielding
College of Arms:	since about 1460, the custodian of the genealogies and armorial bearings of those persons entitled to them
Knights Templar:	an order of twelfth-century crusaders suppressed by the Pope in 1312
morions:	high-crested helmets

| Indian powwow: | Indian priest and conjuror, called also the medicine man |
| Lapland wizard: | a male witch from Lapland |

Chapter 23: The Revelation of the Scarlet Letter

This is the moment of the minister's crisis. He finishes his sermon and walks to the scaffold, where he shows the people his own scarlet letter.

NOTES AND GLOSSARY:

So arrives the greatest crisis of the story. Both the forces of love and of public pressure are at their utmost pitch. The minister has become the central character, as Hester and Chillingworth have made their choices and can only await their fates. Each tempts the minister, one to love, and the other to power. To each, he has surrendered. But now each wants a final act of allegiance, and he cannot give it to both. As he finishes his sermon, the minister tells his people of New England's high purpose and destiny. He speaks to them as the makers of a New World community in special relationship with God. The people feel privileged to hear him. They sense too that he is speaking to them for the last time, giving them his best thought, and urging them to spiritual zeal with all his own real fervour. When he finishes, there is a moment's silence.

> He stood, at this moment, on the very proudest eminence of superiority, to which the gifts of intellect, rich lore, prevailing eloquence, and a reputation of whitest sanctity, could exalt a clergyman in New England's earliest days, when the professional character was of itself a lofty pedestal. Such was the position which the minister occupied, as he bowed his head forward on the cushions of the pulpit, at the close of his Election Sermon.

As the procession moves out, the minister is cheered. His strength seems to fade and he looks ready to collapse. He comes to the scaffold where Hester stands with Pearl. The Governor notices Dimmesdale pausing, and so does the crowd. Dimmesdale calls to Hester and Pearl, in weakness but with a sad triumphant tenderness. Pearl hugs him, Hester moves toward him, and Roger Chillingworth starts to move through the crowd toward them. The doctor tempts Dimmesdale for the last time.

> 'Madman, hold! what is your purpose?' whispered he. 'Wave back that woman! Cast off this child! All shall be well! Do not blacken your fame, and perish in dishonor!'

The temptation of power can only be escaped with the help of love. So the minister asks Hester to support him as he climbs the scaffold. He wants her approval: '"Is this not better," murmured he, "than what we

dreamed of in the forest?"'. Hester is confused. She has heard
Chillingworth mutter 'Hadst thou sought the whole earth over . . . there
was no one place so secret, – no high place nor lowly place, where thou
couldst have escaped me, – save on this very scaffold!' but she longed for
a life of natural fulfilment. She senses this subtle choice is not just self-
revelation, but death. The crowd is rapt, knowing they are witnessing
the minister's most significant testimony.

> People of New England! . . . ye, that have loved me! – ye, that have
> deemed me holy! – behold me here, the one sinner of the world! At
> last! – at last! I stand upon the spot where, seven years since, I should
> have stood; here, with this woman, whose arm, more than the little
> strength wherewith I have crept hitherward, sustains me at this
> dreadful moment, from grovelling down upon my face. Lo, the scarlet
> letter which Hester wears! Ye have all shuddered at it! Wherever her
> walk hath been, – wherever, so miserably burdened, she may have
> hoped to find repose, – it hath cast a lurid gleam of awe and horrible
> repugnance round about her. But there stood one in the midst of you,
> at whose brand of sin and infamy ye have not shuddered! . . . It was on
> him! . . . God's eye beheld it! . . . Behold a dreadful witness of it!

He opens his shirt to show them the brand. Then he sinks down on the
scaffold to die. Hester holds his head against her heart. Chillingworth
says, 'Thou hast escaped me!' and Dimmesdale chides him, 'May God
forgive thee! . . . Thou, too, hast deeply sinned!'. Then he speaks to
Pearl, asking for her love. Pearl's isolation is broken as she sorrowfully
kisses her father. Lastly the minister says his good-bye to Hester.

> Hush, Hester, hush! . . . The law we broke! – the sin here so awfully
> revealed! – let these alone be in thy thoughts! I fear! I fear! It may be
> that, when we forgot our God, – when we violated our reverence each
> for the other's soul, – it was thenceforth vain to hope that we could
> meet hereafter, in an everlasting and pure reunion. God knows; and
> He is merciful! He hath proved his mercy, most of all in my afflictions.
> By giving me this burning torture to bear upon my breast! By sending
> yonder dark and terrible old man, to keep the torture always at red-
> heat! By bringing me hither, to die this death of triumphant ignominy
> before the people! Had either of these agonies been wanting, I had
> been lost forever! Praised be His name! His will be done! Farewell!

With these words, he dies.

clangor:	(in some editions *clamour*) harsh, ringing sound
apotheosized:	deified
meridian:	midpoint, that is, it is a little past mid-day

Chapter 24: Conclusion

In the final chapter Hawthorne contrasts the real story he has told with the tales the townspeople will tell of these events as time goes by. He also adds a few clues as to the fates of the other three main characters: Chillingworth, Hester, and Pearl.

NOTES AND GLOSSARY:

Hawthorne reports that after a time, no one account of what had happened that fateful day could be accepted by all witnesses. Some claimed to have seen a scarlet letter imprinted in the minister's flesh, whether by his own punishing hand, or by the evil doctor's necromancy, or by 'the ever-active tooth of remorse, gnawing from the inmost heart outwardly, and at last manifesting Heaven's dreadful judgment by the presence of the letter'. Others say that they saw nothing. They take the minister's gesture to mean that the most holy man is no better than the scarlet-lettered woman. From these various interpretations Hawthorne selects none, but draws one moral:

> Among many morals which press upon us from the poor minister's miserable experience, we put only this into a sentence: 'Be true! Be true! Be true! Show freely to the world, if not your worst, yet some trait whereby the worst may be inferred!'

After Dimmesdale's death, Chillingworth withers away, his involvement with the minister having been his only hold on life. Hawthorne comments on their relationship.

> It is a curious subject of observation and inquiry, whether hatred and love be not the same thing at bottom. Each, in its utmost development, supposes a high degree of intimacy and heart-knowledge; each renders one individual dependent for the food of his affections and spiritual life upon another; each leaves the passionate lover, or the no less passionate hater, forlorn and desolate by the withdrawal of his subject. Philosophically considered, therefore, the two passions seem essentially the same, except that one happens to be seen in a celestial radiance, and the other in a dusky and lurid glow. In the spiritual world, the old physician and the minister – mutual victims as they have been – may, unawares, have found their earthly stock of hatred and antipathy transmuted into golden love.

Chillingworth's fortune passes to Pearl. She and her mother go away, living somewhere in the old world to which Hester had hoped to bring Dimmesdale. But Hester returns to her lonely cottage in New England, and to the wearing of the scarlet letter, when Pearl has grown and married. There she lives an unselfish life for which people come to respect and trust her. Hawthorne suggests that she needs to return to the place where her life had been lived in its most crucial years, and reports that eventually she was buried with her lover. However, he also relates that Hester had come to see herself as a forerunner of a time when 'a new truth would be revealed, in order to establish the whole relation between man and woman on a surer ground of mutual happiness'.

nugatory: worthless

Part 3

Commentary

Structure

The Scarlet Letter is a complex and beautiful work. Close scrutiny reveals the density of the writing, the enmeshing of ideas and words so closely that each new page further unfolds the themes of the book. It hovers between the structure of a novel and that of an allegory. Hawthorne called it an 'allegorical romance'. Its overall plan is dictated by the *theme* of the story, that is by its expressed and implied meaning. This matters more to Hawthorne than the sequence of actions and events, or *plot*. Hawthorne called it allegorical in the respect that each character, each event, and even each setting correspond to a more abstract idea, and the inter-actions between characters express the inter-actions between ideas as much as between persons.

Where characters live implies something about their destinies; for example, Hester Prynne lives outside the town, and is mentally and spiritually estranged from it. Dimmesdale lives in a rented room, which indicates his utter loneliness. Other places are significant in the story, as closer study will show. The jailhouse, the scaffold, the woods, each correspond to one way a character might relate to his society. A character moving from one place to another is thinking of changing his state of being, as when the Reverend Dimmesdale seeks the scaffold in the dead of night.

Events indicate a development in the inner lives of characters. For Hester, seeing her husband Chillingworth is the occasion of a full, fearful realisation that her adultery will have grim consequences; Chillingworth moving in with Dimmesdale brings with him the shadow of a hopeless remorse, to haunt the young minister. Hawthorne controls the slow development of the story, so that a reader has time to understand what a character's situation means, before an event occurs to change that situation. In this way, the theme, rather than the plot, determines the pace of the story.

Relatively little action is necessary to the writer's purpose, but some action is needed. Each main character is confronted by a moral choice. Each must choose what to value in life, what to reject. So Hawthorne must confront each with a need for action that will make public what values are dear to him or her. Throughout the story Dimmesdale is torn by conflicting desires; he wants to continue his work as preacher and minister, and he wants to confess to the community that he is an adulterer. He cannot do both, he must choose which is the deeper need. Hester's pregnancy, while her husband was away, had made it plain to all that she had sinned before the story opens, but she, too, has a dilemma. She can identify Dimmesdale as her partner in adultery or she can try to protect his good name by her silence. In rejecting the community's right to know her partner's name, she is refusing to acknowledge their right to punish adultery. As many critics have observed, Hester remains unrepentant throughout the story. Chillingworth, Hester's wronged husband, also has a moral choice. He has arrived in the town unrecognised except by Hester, who is prepared to keep his identity secret. He can use this strange situation for good or evil. He can relate to Hester and Dimmesdale in a benign or a malevolent bond. He chooses private revenge, and begins to live for hate.

These three central characters find their lives made stark and diminished. The ordinary complexity of life fades from their minds and feelings. They are left with lives of appalling clarity and simple definition, as when a skeleton is all that remains of what was once a man. Allegory does tend to reduce characters to simplified types in this way, but Hawthorne's approach is more subtle. Through the course of the book he tries to suggest full-blooded people aware their community is turning them into allegorical figures. Hester is the scapegoat, who bears her role as unwillingly as any simple, natural creature would. Dimmesdale was the church leader; he already filled a symbolic role for the people. He resists, and only gradually accepts, his change of role from that to punished sinner. But, in the closing chapter when he desires the new role and seeks it, the community cannot believe his life is not, and does not mean, what they took it to be and to mean. The most curious of the three adult central characters is Chillingworth. He opts for a simplification of his life willingly and privately, and the community only gradually senses that he acts as an agent of destruction. Yet in a sense he too is their victim, for he has accepted their evaluation of adultery as terrible, punishable sin. The fourth central character, Pearl, comes close to representing the 'natural child' of a love outside marriage, and even the living emblem of the scarlet letter. Pearl is unconscious of this.

Allegorical writing is formal and often constructed in symmetries. This story is so constructed around three scaffold scenes. In the first Hester, beautiful and sorrowful, clutches the infant to whom she has given life, standing under the severe public gaze. It is broad daylight and a number of people watch, including the public representatives who officially inflict this disgrace. She wears the scarlet letter A embroidered on her dress to signify her adultery. She is condemned always to wear it as a mark of shame. Yet she has embroidered it beautifully in her sad defiance and her muted assertion of her own dignity. Her child suffers with her; they are isolated from their neighbours. Hawthorne ruefully compares them to Jesus and Mary. In doing so he does not reject the notion of adultery as wrong but shows a compassion that respects the privacy of the wrongdoer. This first scaffold scene raises the central question of the book: ought sin always to be made public and publicly punished? Can it not be safely left to the person's private self to weigh up his acts and judge? Hawthorne values 'the sanctity of the human heart' and fears the hypocrisy of any man assuming he knows another so well, and is himself so righteous, that he can judge someone else's deed. Though Hawthorne makes this aversion plain, he also communicates a respect for society's need to enforce some standards.

If the first scaffold scene alerts the reader to this complex thought of Hawthorne's, the second scaffold scene enlarges and sustains it. Dimmesdale needs public confession; private penance is not enough. The minister also carries the burden of his society's need for a publicly active agent of righteousness who will again and again exhort them to moral effort, and will stir them by his own example. The scaffold is willingly mounted by the distraught minister even before Hester and Pearl come up to join him. However, it is dead of night and the good people of the town do not see Dimmesdale's act of confession. Even the Reverend Wilson, passing by the scaffold with a lantern does not pick out the lonely figure in the dark. Even then Dimmesdale is not left to his private world. Two people in Governor Bellingham's mansion have heard his shriek of anguish, the Governor himself and his sister, Mistress Hibbins. They see nothing when they come to their windows. When the minister laughs hysterically, his daughter Pearl laughs in an answering merriment, and thus leads Dimmesdale to call out to her. While Hester and Pearl stand with him, the three are seen by Chillingworth, who will keep secret what he has seen for his own greater extortion of revenge. Chillingworth leads the minister home, but Dimmesdale has dropped a glove on the scaffold, which will be found by an ordinary townsman. Discovery thus comes close to Dimmesdale but does not quite overtake him.

In this second scaffold scene, supernatural forces are at work, diverting the reader from the psychological struggle of the minister to the moral backdrop. The sky is emblazoned by a large red letter A; Chillingworth could not have seen the three except for its light. Other people who see the letter mistake it for a sign that dying Governor Winthrop is becoming an angel, a pure spirit about to enter joyfully into God's immediate presence. The finder of Dimmesdale's glove next morning also reckons it a supernatural theft by Satan. These readings come naturally to people who believe the world is imbued with the activity of good and evil spirits. However, Hawthorne's ambivalence is made plain; the red A does light up the sky, but the townspeople mistake its meaning. Not Satan, but a guilt-ridden human being dropped the glove on the scaffold. Good and evil exist, and may manifest themselves in strange and almost magical ways, but they are independent of human judgement, which often errs.

The strange events give this scene in *The Scarlet Letter* the air of fairy tale or romance. In such works, magical laws are as dependable as scientific laws, and as independent of the wills of human characters. But in Hawthorne's writing it is *moral laws* which often manifest themselves suddenly and in strange ways. Truth about characters's moral lives becomes plain as if by magical power (and in this case, aided by a supernatural sign). Because the story has been consistently true to common life until this point, the extraordinary event hovers between allegory and magic. Hawthorne's casual asides about witchcraft in this scene heighten this effect because they imply that perhaps he himself is a believer in magic.

The third scaffold scene is even more intense. References to a magic circle within which Hester is isolated with Pearl, prepare the reader for the world of ordinary life being intruded upon by greater powers. Mistress Hibbins, the witch, approaches Hester to speak of Dimmesdale's secret, but opposed to the dark magic is the power of Dimmesdale's sermon, in which he begs the congregation to commit themselves to belief in God's power, and to subject themselves to God's moral laws. As the people listen, they come almost to regard the minister as an angel of light, God's special emissary to their community. He asks them not just as individuals, but as a community, to dedicate their lives to God's purpose, living out a moral example that will shine forth in a sinful world, and convert other communities. Then after leaving the church, the minister calls Hester and Pearl to him. They have waited outside the church as if they have no role in this kingdom of God on earth that the minister speaks of, yet he calls to them. Chillingworth emerges from the crowd, like the dark power wanting to destroy Dimmesdale and his work, but he admits defeat when the minister climbs the scaffold.

Dimmesdale wishes to be redeemed from the evil power to which his hypocrisy has bonded him. To become free he must act; he must reveal his hidden adultery. This he does, by opening his shirt and revealing to everyone a red A burned into his flesh. He speaks to them with great anguish, telling them all of his sin. The effort proves fatal, and he sinks down into Hester's arms, dying. He asks Pearl for a kiss, and in kissing him, she is filled with grief. Her isolation is broken, her wild independent nature begins to tame itself to human sympathies. Hester looks for some natural solace. If they cannot live together on earth, surely a shared afterlife will be theirs. But the minister is not so sure, and leaves her without any real consolation. The seemingly supernatural A that appears on the minister's chest cannot be seen by everyone and its true significance is grasped by only a few. Some take it as a self-inflicted penance, others as a mark Chillingworth has inflicted through black magic; a few make the judgement that the minister's spiritual suffering has been gradually expressed by his body in a supernatural way. With this confusion the story returns to its original theme, that all lives are ultimately secret and cannot be fully penetrated by any outsider. The human heart scarcely knows its own motives fully. Only the divine Creator knows the real inner life a person leads.

In discussing the basic structure of *The Scarlet Letter* this section has argued that the action is minimal, and always corresponds to emotional or moral changes in the characters's lives. The characters' inter-relationships are determined by an over-riding concern they all share, a concern with the meaning of adulterous wrongdoing and its punishment. Despite their complex humanity, they become allegorical figures. Firstly, they are such to their community. However, the community's interpretations are often wrong. Secondly, and more profoundly, they each begin to see themselves and one another allegorically. However, finally, Hawthorne thinks even this is presumption. He leaves intact the mystery of each person.

Theme

Because of this approach of Hawthorne's, *The Scarlet Letter* is more than a plainly allegorical work. The writer will not identify any one character as hero or heroine, nor will he allow any character to achieve a monopoly of wisdom. The truth, in as much as it emerges, will be shadowy and ambivalent, a matter for private judgement by each reader. This is a Romantic view of truth, that each person finds his own 'truth' and virtue consists in living in correspondence with its insight. Still, Hawthorne implies that these individual apprehensions of truth may not cancel out an ultimate standard of right and wrong. He is concerned that men jump prematurely to moral judgements of one another, and even of themselves. He does not want to abandon moral standards; he wants to sensitise them.

Such a complex theme requires a writer to present a variety of complex moral situations. Hawthorne has done this by using a group of central characters, rather than a single hero or heroine. In this way complexity of expression is possible; each situation is seen from the different characters's points of view. Hawthorne makes full use of this.

Critics frequently refer to Hawthorne's ambivalence and subtlety. By this they mean an ability to suggest that the meaning of events will seem different to different readers. One reader may emphasise Hawthorne's repulsion from hypocrisy as he portrays it in Dimmesdale and in the even more unquestioning hypocrisy of the community at large. Another reader may see an overall structure like a Greek tragedy, in which a noble figure, Dimmesdale, is ruined by a flaw or sin, while a chorus watches only half-comprehendingly. A third reader may consider the story as primarily Hester's tale of men with artificial standards oppressing a natural, life-giving woman. *The Scarlet Letter* itself contains hints of each of these interpretations. The ambivalence is the presence of these various possible meanings within the story; the subtlety is the author's skill in including each without quite obliterating or erasing any of the others. Because the author is mainly concerned with theme, the writing is close to allegory despite its ideas being open to various interpretations. The personal histories of the main characters do not seem to interest the author, except as they bear on the meaning of their relationship to the punishment for adultery. The simplicity of plot, or sequence of events, is contrasted with the complexity of theme; events are selected for depiction if they bear on the theme, left out if they do not. Therefore, the reader may look for a purpose in the inclusion of each scene, more intently than he usually may in fiction.

Language

The language Hawthorne uses in *The Scarlet Letter* is closer to the language of poetry than to a clear prose style. Hawthorne does not linger over lengthy descriptions and explanations. For example, in describing places he quickly passes over physical descriptions and uses suggestive words to imply a place's emotional effect on one or more of the main characters. This can be seen in the following passage:

> A clump of scrubby trees, such as alone grew on the peninsula, did not so much conceal the cottage from view, as seem to denote that here was some object which would fain have been, or at least ought to be, concealed. In this little lonesome dwelling, with some slender means that she possessed, and by the licence of the magistrates, who still kept an inquisitorial watch over her, Hester established herself with her infant child. (Chapter 5).

This fusing of physical details with emotional impressions is a poetic technique that Hawthorne uses extensively. Here are two more examples:

> Certain it is, that, some fifteen or twenty years after the settlement of the town, the wooden jail was already marked with weather-stains and other indications of age, which gave a yet darker aspect to its beetle-browed and gloomy front. The rust on the ponderous iron-

work of its oaken door looked more antique than anything else in the New World. Like all that pertains to crime, it seemed never to have known a youthful era. (Chapter 1).

The sportive sunlight – feebly sportive, at best, in the predominant pensiveness of the day and scene – withdrew itself as they came nigh, and left the spots where it had danced the drearier, because they had hoped to find them bright. (Chapter 16).

In the little world of the story, nature responds sympathetically to the main characters' feelings. When Hester and Dimmesdale first sit down together in the forest,

the forest was obscure around them, and creaked with a blast that was passing through it. The boughs were tossing heavily above their heads; while one solemn old tree groaned dolefully to another, as if telling the sad story of the pair that sat beneath, or constrained to forebode evil to come. (Chapter 17).

The terrible storm on the night when Dimmesdale stands on the scaffold and the midday brightness that illumines his full confession reflect his feelings. Making nature respond like this gives it animistic vitality; it seems spiritually, as well as physically alive. Hawthorne suggests particularly how close Pearl and Hester are to nature; they belong more to the world of nature than to the world of men. To some extent, Hawthorne seems to approve of this, and in that degree he is a Romantic. Nineteenth-century Romantic writers often spoke of society as an artificial constraint on human activity that killed spontaneity and sincerity. While Hawthorne may see the need for social order, he does make us feel the opposition between natural spontaneity and social restriction.

One way he does this is by contrasting the animistic language he uses to describe nature with the formal language spoken by most of his characters. Dimmesdale especially uses a very formal kind of speech even in his most private conversations. A striking example of this is his reaction to Hester's revelation that Chillingworth is her wronged husband. His language blooms with rhetoric like a dark and stunted flower:

'I might have known it,' murmured he. 'I did know it! Was not the secret told me, in the natural recoil of my heart at the first sight of him, and as often as I have seen him since? Why did I not understand? O Hester Prynne, thou little, little knowest all the horror of this thing! And the shame! – the indelicacy! – the horrible ugliness of this exposure of a sick and guilty heart to the very eye that would gloat over it! Woman, woman, thou art accountable for this! I cannot forgive thee! (Chapter 17).

Pearl's is the most simple and direct speech of anyone's in the story. However, Pearl tends to be silent more often than her mother wishes and is inclined to say strange and unexpected things. Hawthorne shows us that this gives Hester a great deal of worry and grief. It provokes crises in their lives. Because of Pearl's strange reply to Governor Bellingham's question 'Who made thee?' Pearl is very nearly lost to Hester and put in someone else's care. Because Pearl will not speak sweetly to Dimmesdale, no easy reconciliation of her father with her mother is possible. Pearl's speech is disconcerting. Even when she is telling about her imaginings, she reveals directly and simply what is on her mind. Hawthorne demonstrates that this Romantic behaviour has one sad drawback: Pearl hurts other people, most especially her mother.

Thus, although the contrast Hawthorne is making between natural and restricted speech is one the Romantics made, Hawthorne does not idealise the natural as much as they did. He recognises that people must control their words carefully and sensitively if they are not to injure others. He exemplifies this in Hester's speech. Hester has learned not always to say what she thinks, even if it means that she must often lapse into silence. When she does speak, she governs herself strictly. Partly she does this to protect herself and Pearl from further insult. Partly she does it to protect Dimmesdale. Often Hester's silences are effective. For a long time she is silent about Chillingworth being her husband; she never says to anyone that Dimmesdale was once her lover.

Hawthorne shows us the dark side of deliberately controlling speech in Chillingworth. Chillingworth misuses words to create false impressions, even to the extent of giving himself a false name. The cruel doctor almost always says the expected thing, he is frank only three times in the story: when he confronts Hester in prison, when he and Hester meet years later, and when he admits defeat as Dimmesdale stands on the scaffold with Hester and Pearl. The rest of the time his speech is smooth and superficially pious, a surface of lies covering a terrible anger. The last time Chillingworth is alone with Dimmesdale, a reader realises how lying has become almost a compulsion for him. Even though he recognises that the minister knows his real identity, and is aware of the dark menace behind his care, Chillingworth continues to utter pious pleasantries, to which the minister responds in kind.

'Verily, dear sir, we must take pains to make you strong and vigorous for this occasion of the Election discourse. The people look for great things from you; apprehending that another year may come about and find their pastor gone.'

'Yes, to another world,' replied the minister, with pious resignation. 'Heaven grant it be a better one; for, in good sooth, I hardly think to tarry with my flock through the flitting seasons of another year!' (Chapter 20)

This scene shows the minister at his most hypocritical. He is almost blasphemous in speaking of going to a new world beyond death when he really intends to run off to the Old World of Europe with Hester and Pearl. Again, he betrays his ministry in his ironic promise to repay Chillingworth's 'good deeds' with his prayers. Chillingworth abets this terrible lying with false gratitude.

Left to himself after this, Dimmesdale rewrites his Election Sermon. Hawthorne does not tell the reader more than that he is dissatisfied with the first draft and works all night on a new version. His spiritual language is revitalised by his contact with Hester, and given such power that at some point in writing or delivering his sermon, he re-converts himself to religious purpose.

Thus in each character's speech is manifested a terrific respect for the power of words. Hawthorne has described a community which believes that God's revelation is primarily verbal, and that the study of God's word, the Bible, is the main route to salvation. He has shown that this community expects good lives to be fundamentally directed by the verbal guidance of a religious leader who in his preaching guides the development of the society as a whole, as well as its individual members. However, he also warns that a second power, which some call magic and some call evil, opposes the first. It also uses words. The Black Man wants people to write their names in his Book. People committed to this other destructive power use lies as a way of protecting themselves and gaining control over others. Poised between these powers shiver the individual souls of Hester, Dimmesdale, and Pearl.

Characterisation

There are four main characters in *The Scarlet Letter*: Hester Prynne; Arthur Dimmesdale; Roger Chillingworth; and Pearl.

Hester

All through the story Hester is under great stress. She is never able to express her own nature fully, but the author offers hints of the sort of woman she is. The fate which befell her before the novel opens suggests that she is reckless and passionate. In the first scaffold scene, when Hester is holding the infant Pearl as she stands on the pillory platform, her thoughts return to the anxiety her own mother had felt for her. Her marriage was reckless and made more in a spirit of adventure than in love. She travelled away from her family, first to Amsterdam, and then, without her husband, to the New World. This suggests that her independent energy had struck even Chillingworth. Many a dutiful wife would have waited till her husband could accompany her, but Hester did not feel that duty or that need, not did her husband insist that she should wait for him.

Her love for Dimmesdale was consummated in an act of love both passionate and reckless. Although traditionally women are more cautious than men in sexual love, Hester was perhaps more heedless than Dimmesdale. However, Hester shows great courage in accepting the consequences of her own deeds. She asks no one for sympathy or help. Hester's courageous reaction to her terrible predicament shows that her values are quite different from those dear to the Massachusetts colony. They value a moulding of people into a rigid social order. Hester is a radical individualist.

This does not mean that she takes no responsibility for anyone else. She is extraordinarily loyal to Dimmesdale and Pearl. She does not allow her sad story to embitter her love for them, although it taints the rest of her feelings.

Dimmesdale

Arthur Dimmesdale is a lonely individual, as Hester is, but Hawthorne describes more of what goes on in his troubled mind than he does in the case of Hester. His struggle between the desire to continue in his ministry and his natural moral feeling that he should share Hester's shame costs him great suffering, for he is basically an honourable, simple man. He cannot bear a contradiction between his private assessment of his acts, and the public's opinion of him. However, throughout the whole story he is revealed to be a man to whom work and the public role are more important that private affections. Gradually, he comes to believe that his private life can be reconciled with his public work by a complete confession, a final act which casts away all hope of a shared happiness with Hester and Pearl. He is as sure that public life is more important that private, as Hester is that private life is more important than public.

Although this difference in values divides them, they are alike in other ways. Like Hester, Dimmesdale has courage. Like her, he is ultimately true to the values he understands. Both are 'good' characters whose vision of life, however painfully, enlarges beyond the narrow view of their fellow townsfolk.

Dimmesdale is a scholar trained for his ministry by a study of Biblical languages and a close study of the Biblical text. The Puritans saw themselves as restoring the Christian tradition to its original purity by confining theology to Biblical analysis. They were not trying to create a new faith but to restore an old one. They hoped to inspire whole communities with zeal for Christian living, mainly through powerful preaching and Bible study. Dimmesdale represents many of their best virtues. He is conscientious, learned, and eager to serve. He also represents some of their common vices. He is hypocritical, humourless, and a bit vain.

He is contrasted with the man of science, Chillingworth, whose possible virtues and apparent vices are quite different.

Chillingworth

Chillingworth is a perverse man of science. Even his name suggests his moral destiny: all real worth in him is chilled by his lack of interest in ordinary human relationships. When, late in life, he marries a passionate young girl, he cannot satisfy her. Her unfaithfulness does thaw his emotions, but only to a heat of revenge. No anguish or regret troubles him. No complex feelings are within him. His only mental habits, singlemindedness and quizzical experimentation, take on sinister purpose. He experiments in revenge. He invents new tortures. Allowing nothing to distract him, he has nothing to save him from the evil in himself. Moreover, he has nothing to live for when revenge is done.

Romantic writers such as William Wordsworth (1770–1850) and Samuel Taylor Coleridge (1772–1834) had as little use for the new science as they had for traditional pious practice. They feared its claim to free reason from emotion, believing that this would rob man of his greatest power, an intuitive energy of mind that understands what emotional experiences mean. Chillingworth is such a man, who for all he discovers, learns nothing. Lost to him is his wife and lost the children she might have borne him, lost, too, is the real friendship he might have had with a man such as Dimmesdale. A reader senses the loss, but Chillingworth does not, and he does not grieve over his own fate.

Because Chillingworth dedicates himself to revenge early in the tale, it is easy to view him as a 'bad' character. However, Hawthorne allows his readers inklings of the good energies that are wasted by Chillingworth's choice. For his disinterestedness might have been noble if he had remained tied to human sympathies. If even a general compassion for people had moved him more deeply, he might have been an able and innovative physician. Chillingworth is someone whose emotional famine ends in a dark feast of revenge. This makes him a figure of black magic in Hawthorne's sense, that is, someone who has willingly committed his soul to the devil's care, and who becomes learned in the arts of evil-doing. Few writers have such a strong sense as Hawthorne had, that evil practice, like goodness, is learned very slowly, degree by degree, until it pervades a person's whole will. Hawthorne had a Puritan conviction that the choice of a good or an evil life may well be made in a moment, and then be irreversible, but he saw it then as a subtle force that gradually took over an individual's personality.

Pearl

Pearl is a character who has not yet chosen good or evil. She is in a natural pre-moral state. In this crucial sense she is an unformed person and a reader cannot penetrate much of her personality. Her innocence is tainted with a natural inclination to selfishness, perhaps strengthened by her sadly solitary life. Hawthorne tries to show that Pearl is like a rippling stream, mirroring life around her without really understanding or judging it for herself. She is as free of ties as Chillingworth is, and is in moral peril for that reason.

Hester tries to draw Pearl's affections to herself, but the child needs to experience a range of emotional attachments if she is to learn to love. Her love for her mother is dependence. This cruel fact is brought home to Hester when Pearl insists that she put back the scarlet letter she had cast aside to share an hour's peace with Dimmesdale.

Pearl's crisis, at the end of the story, is really a reaction to the crisis of her parents. However, for the first time in her life, she sees their needs, and realises that she herself has something to give. Hawthorne suggests that this is the beginning of her moral life. Her later life is only sketchily suggested in the chapter called 'Conclusion' but the author implies that she lives as an adult with the colour and passion denied to Hester. This would suit Pearl, whose imagination and courage are natural gifts needing only discipline, not cultivation.

The place of magic in the story

Hawthorne's ambivalent use of magical incidents makes it almost impossible for a reader to be sure how seriously the author takes the supernatural. Hawthorne complicates this by setting the story in the past, and then suggesting that long ago magical forces were more powerful than in his own time. Moreover, the real power comes from the undisturbed, primeval forest whose memory of the deep and lost past gives it an identity that can envelop and overpower individuals who enter it. The use of a special place where the power of magic dominates the power of reason is part of Hawthorne's structural allegory. He is implying that a person in the forest senses in his or her own soul a special corresponding place where passion and deep desires play the tunes and reason dances. This may seem complicated or difficult to a reader when talked about by a critic, but it can be taken in easily enough when reading the story.

Some of the magic is almost benevolent, like the renewing power the forest exerts on Hester and Dimmesdale in the chapter 'A Flood of Sunshine'. In Pearl's intuitive understanding of magic, however, we see both its light and shade. It makes her inventive and lively, but it also allows her to be domineering. Magic is a sympathy with nature that makes someone powerful, in ways that can interfere with the rightful privacy of others. Using magical power can also violate natural modesty, in an individual's desire to exert control for his own ends. Such sins against natural reserve offend Hawthorne deeply, for his chief belief is 'the sanctity of the human heart'.

Summation

Hawthorne's achievement in *'The Scarlet Letter'*

The Scarlet Letter is a remarkable book; its acute insight and quiet economy give it great force. The poetic beauty of much of the language creates the book's warmth and colour. A reader might expect that the moral energy of the writer would be splayed and lost because of the complexity of his thought, but this does not happen, because in every respect except theme the book is simple and strong. The action is so economically constructed that no incident is peripheral; the characters are few, and simply drawn. The events of the story seem to be put before the reader in various lights and seasons of the heart. This gives the book the real quality of looking on at something living, seeing it at different times of day, or seasons of the year, and in the end sensing its mystery and selfhood.

Hawthorne distances these events in time, so that the reader knows even more surely that he cannot reach or affect them, even with anger. They have the quietness of the unreachable past, which defies judgement and involvement. Hawthorne thus achieves the stance he wants, as an observer who cares but does not interfere, one who will think about what the story means with his public as he narrates the tale, but will modestly conclude that they may have their own opinions. Hawthorne is like the writer in *The Blithedale Romance* who sensed that he had

> that quality of the intellect and the heart which impelled me (often against my own will, and to the detriment of my own comfort) to live in other lives, and to endeavour – by generous sympathies, by delicate intuitions, by taking note of things too slight for record, and by bringing my human spirit into manifold accordance with the companions whom God assigned me – to learn the secret which was hidden even from themselves.

This basic attitude to his work motivates a search for appropriate forms in which to write; this leads to the allegorical romance, a new form of his own invention. The soothing voice of a storyteller in a rocking chair is adopted, but the exploration of life going on in the teller's tale is never soft and cosy. He has a troubled mind; he wants to talk about things happening that he feels even conventional religion does not deal with, those guilts that are hidden from it and innocences that are misunderstood. Hawthorne is a daring writer who does not relish being daring. He cloaks it with great courtesy to his subject and to his readers. This diffidence does not prevent them from realising what Hawthorne values *in general*: he values a generous blooming life that after it flowers is willing to be harvested – life that both wants to be alive in its own right, and wants to pass on something useful to other lives. The dark creed of his Puritan ancestors has cast its shadow over him: he believes people tend naturally to lose their way, often making mistakes that only superhuman effort can redeem. They become wise after the fact, sometimes only for sorrow, sometimes for redemption. Hawthorne is no Romantic, although he uses sensitivity to animated nature to enlarge his own portfolio of paintings. He wants to say things they would never say. He takes no comfort in the companionship of other minds, not hiding from the rain of wisdom in a forest of friendly nature, or among fellow men, but only, like that writer in *The Blithedale Romance*, climbing a tree from which he can see life at a distance and in a safe seclusion. However, the castle that another educated innocent climbs (*The Marble Faun*) is not just a heap of human building but a vantage point from which to see the changing sky, and wonder at its myriad sun and shade cast on the earth.

What Hawthorne does not know affects him as deeply as what he thinks he knows, in two ways. The first is negative. He never knows all the details of a character's deeds and will not, like almost any other fiction writer, invent them. What he does not know then is like a lingering aftertaste that cannot be defined as a flavour. What he does not feel convinced about metaphysically affects him positively. He is unsure that life is sad and even has glimmerings that it is not. Hawthorne believes that the pure in heart can know a little what the real intended beauty of life is, but that no one is very pure in heart. He hopes that life means something wonderful. He hopes that it is cared for by a fatherly God whose strictness improves his love. Hawthorne values the domestic greatly, and wants the universe to be a domestic place. That happy side of this man's life made him feel that the pattern of any real happiness for people was the pattern of home. Perhaps even then, at life's end, he wanted a God to converse with, rather than a God of settled opinions, a fragile God compared to Calvin's, but a more interesting one.

Part 4

Hints for study

Points for detailed study

1. The vocabulary in *The Scarlet Letter* is quite difficult. You will need to keep a dictionary handy. Notice, too, that the language is formal. Some of it is Biblical or theological. If you look for this, you will find your understanding of the language enriched.

2. Every scene in *The Scarlet Letter* is essential. When you read a scene ask yourself why it is important. The basic structure of the book is sketched for you in Part 3 of these Notes; ask yourself how a scene fits into this structure.

3. In an allegorical romance each character, even a minor character, signifies something beyond his or her own personality. Each has a part to play in telling you the author's ideas. Try to comprehend what the character's deeper reference is, when you analyse each character.

4. Hawthorne wants you to enjoy the experience of imaginatively re-entering the past. Do it with an open mind. Allow yourself time to consider the society he is describing. Let your imagination picture the landscape and climate as you do this, so that you sense the physical side of life in that society. Think of the different work in which characters are involved, and of what their daily life would be like.

5. The supernatural seems significant to Hawthorne. Find out what you can about witchcraft in seventeenth century New England. Is Hawthorne portraying it accurately, or has he changed it in some way to make it fit and appeal to the nineteenth-century opinions of his first readers?

6. As a romance, the book achieves a certain atmosphere of 'long ago and far away'. This makes the book more entertaining. How do you think the story would seem in a modern setting? What would it lose, and/or gain?

7. Good and evil oppose each other dramatically in the book. First make a list of 'good' characters and then one of 'bad' characters. But Hawthorne is a subtle writer. Ask yourself what trace of badness is in each 'good' character, what goodness might be developed in each 'bad' character. If you work hard at this, you will begin to see the complexity of Hawthorne's theme.

8. The final scaffold scene is the greatest crisis of the book. It comes as a surprise, as we had expected Dimmesdale to run away with Hester and Pearl. Think about why Dimmesdale changed his mind. You might even try writing a monologue on his thoughts. Think also about how the crisis has been prepared for in the two chapters preceding.

Specimen questions and answers

When you come to answer examination questions on *The Scarlet Letter* you may find that you are being asked to consider the book in a way you had not yet thought of. Do not just write down what you know about the book; instead, re-read the question a few times until you are sure you have thoroughly understood it. Then,

1. Try to ask yourself what you know that might bear on the question. Make a few notes.

2. Re-read your notes, and the question. Build up your notes for a few moments.

3. Take one basic idea from your notes on which to *build your answer*. You may be able to write this down as your opening sentence. Bring in your other material to enlarge on this idea, to show it in sidelights, and even to challenge it and refine it.

4. If you have time, you may similarly develop one or two more ideas. If you do this, connect them to your first idea.

5. Finally, re-read your answer quickly. Add a concluding paragraph, if necessary, to summarise your reply.

Here are a few examples of likely questions, with outlines of possible answers.

Hawthorne says his romances take place in 'a neutral territory between the Actual and the Imaginary'. What does this mean, in terms of *The Scarlet Letter*?

At the simplest level this could be taken as a question about *setting*. Hawthorne has used seventeenth century New England as a neutral territory between the actual and the imaginary. It is actual, but it must be re-created in the imagination.

At another level this could be a question about the author's treatment of characters. They are not just real people, but imagined people who symbolise more than just themselves.

Finally, there are Hawthorne's suggestions of the supernatural. They create a near fairy-tale atmosphere, but they also enrich the moral seriousness of the book.

Hawthorne has four main characters in *The Scarlet Letter*. Is there a hero or heroine?

First, name the four main characters and say why each matters in the story. Then *decide* whether you think one is outstanding among the four. If you do, try to show how focusing on this character clarifies the *theme* of the story.

The Scarlet Letter takes place in a symbolic landscape. Comment.

This kind of question can seem quite frightening as you wonder what to say after you have said 'Yes'. However, it is a very open question; an answer can be developed in a variety of ways. For this reason, *two* specimen answers are given in outline.

The landscape of *The Scarlet Letter* is symbolic in that each place mentioned in the story carries a special meaning for the characters. The forest is a wild place opposed to organised town life. Discuss the conflict between these two as it parallels the basic conflict in the characters's lives. The scaffold seems to represent the clash and painful reconciliation of these two forces. Discuss its meaning in each of the three scaffold scenes. If you have time, you may wish to fill out your answer with reference to a few other places such as Hester's cottage, or Dimmesdale's study.

Here is an alternative answer:

The Scarlet Letter does have a symbolic landscape but the symbols are often ambivalent. In this respect the book is not a straightforward allegory. For example, the isolation of Hester's cottage is a physical fact, symbolising her own isolation. But why is she so isolated? Partly because she chooses to be so, and always did. She was, and remains, a nonconformist in beliefs and behaviour. Another example is Dimmesdale's study, which symbolises his official role and his inheritance of tradition. Its tapestries show both the heavily moral atmosphere, and the settled middle-class conviction that prosperity is God's blessing. In contrast, the forest both renews Dimmesdale's physical vigour and puts his soul in peril. It provides witches with a secret place to hold their coven, but also, in daylight, gives Dimmesdale and Hester their only chance of a private meeting. Each place mentioned seems to mean something really very complicated. Only the scaffold, that symbol of conflict and tyranny, retains its meaning as an instrument of suffering and death. Perhaps a reader should even qualify this by saying that to Dimmesdale it becomes like Jesus's cross, the necessary death for redemption's sake.

In what sense is *The Scarlet Letter* a novel?

The difficulty of this question is the knowledge it requires of other American and English writing. In attempting an answer, you could first briefly give a working definition of a novel, with reference to what you consider to be a couple of typical books. Then you could compare (and contrast) *The Scarlet Letter* with this, showing that it is an extended piece of prose writing which considers deeply the emotional and moral development of a few characters who find themselves in situations needing decision and action for their resolutions. You could, incidentally, point out why it is not a realistic novel of the nineteenth century's favourite kind, and perhaps mention the influence of Scott's romances and Bunyan's *The Pilgrim's Progress* on Hawthorne's mind and work.

Part 5

Suggestions for further reading

The text

The best American text is the Centenary edition of the *Works of Nathaniel Hawthorne,* Ohio State University Press, Columbus, Ohio, 1963. *The Scarlet Letter* is Volume I, edited by William Charrat and others. Previously the standard edition had been the twelve-volume Riverside Edition of *The Complete Works of Nathaniel Hawthorne,* edited by George Lathrop, Houghton Mifflin, Boston, 1883.

A paperback edition of *The Scarlet Letter* is published by J. M. Dent, London 1977, in the Everyman Library series, with an introduction by R. W. Butterfield. There is also a Penguin edition, edited by Thomas Connolly, published by Penguin Books, Harmondsworth in 1971. The reader will find minor textual variations between these editions but none of these are sufficiently serious to affect his study of the story.

Other works by Nathanial Hawthorne

The Complete Novels and Selected Tales of Nathaniel Hawthorne, edited by Norman Holmes Pearson and published by Random House, New York, 1937, is the largest one-volume selection of Hawthorne's work: it includes thirty-six of Hawthorne's tales and sketches. *The Portable Hawthorne,* with an introduction by Malcolm Cowley, The Viking Press, New York, 1948 includes *The Scarlet Letter,* twelve tales and selections from the notebooks and letters. Individual titles have been published in Everyman's Library and by other British publishers who have series of literary classics.

General reading: books about Hawthorne

ARVIN, NEWTON: *Hawthorne,* Little, Brown, Boston, 1929. A good critical biography.

FOGLE, RICHARD: *Hawthorne's Fiction: The Light and the Dark,* University of Oklahoma Press, Norman, revised edition, 1964. A standard critical study which includes an interesting and detailed look at the romances.

HAWTHORNE, JULIAN: *Nathaniel Hawthorne and His Wife*, 2 vols., J. R. Osgood, Boston, 1884. An intimate study of Hawthorne's life by his own son.

JAMES, HENRY: *Hawthorne*, Macmillan, London, 1879. Interesting because of James's own development as a major novelist.

KAUL, A. N. (ed.): *Hawthorne: A Collection of Critical Essays*, Prentice-Hall, Englewood Cliffs, New Jersey, 1966. A sound collection of essays by critics of very disparate viewpoints.

MALE, R. R.: *Hawthorne's Tragic Vision*, University of Texas Press, Austin, 1957; paperback edition W. W. Norton, New York, 1957. A basic critical work on the romances and the tales.

STEWART, RANDALL: *Nathaniel Hawthorne: A Biography*, Yale University Press, New Haven, 1948. The standard biography, which is pleasantly written and very informative.

WAGGONER, HYATT: *Hawthorne: A Critical Study*, Harvard University Press, Cambridge, Mass., 1955, revised edition, 1963. This closely analyses patterns of symbols and images in the tales and the romances.

The author of these notes

SUZANNE BROWN was educated at Mount Holyoke College and Trinity College Dublin, where she took a Diploma in Anglo-Irish literature and a Higher Diploma in Education before working for her Ph.D. in English there. She has lectured at Trinity College in modern English literature. She is a member of the Council for *An Oige Treitheach*, the Irish National Association for Gifted Children. She is the author of York Notes on *Oliver Twist* and *Dombey and Son*.

York Notes: list of titles

CHINUA ACHEBE
A Man of the People
Arrow of God
Things Fall Apart

EDWARD ALBEE
Who's Afraid of Virginia Woolf?

ELECHI AMADI
The Concubine

ANONYMOUS
Beowulf
Everyman

JOHN ARDEN
Serjeant Musgrave's Dance

AYI KWEI ARMAH
The Beautyful Ones Are Not Yet Born

W. H. AUDEN
Selected Poems

JANE AUSTEN
Emma
Mansfield Park
Northanger Abbey
Persuasion
Pride and Prejudice
Sense and Sensibility

HONORÉ DE BALZAC
Le Père Goriot

SAMUEL BECKETT
Waiting for Godot

SAUL BELLOW
Henderson, The Rain King

ARNOLD BENNETT
Anna of the Five Towns

WILLIAM BLAKE
Songs of Innocence, Songs of Experience

ROBERT BOLT
A Man For All Seasons

ANNE BRONTË
The Tenant of Wildfell Hall

CHARLOTTE BRONTË
Jane Eyre

EMILY BRONTË
Wuthering Heights

ROBERT BROWNING
Men and Women

JOHN BUCHAN
The Thirty-Nine Steps

JOHN BUNYAN
The Pilgrim's Progress

BYRON
Selected Poems

ALBERT CAMUS
L'Etranger (The Outsider)

GEOFFREY CHAUCER
Prologue to the Canterbury Tales
The Clerk's Tale
The Franklin's Tale
The Knight's Tale
The Merchant's Tale
The Miller's Tale
The Nun's Priest's Tale
The Pardoner's Tale
The Wife of Bath's Tale
Troilus and Criseyde

ANTON CHEKOV
The Cherry Orchard

SAMUEL TAYLOR COLERIDGE
Selected Poems

WILKIE COLLINS
The Moonstone
The Woman in White

SIR ARTHUR CONAN DOYLE
The Hound of the Baskervilles

WILLIAM CONGREVE
The Way of the World

JOSEPH CONRAD
Heart of Darkness
Lord Jim
Nostromo
The Secret Agent
Victory
Youth and *Typhoon*

STEPHEN CRANE
The Red Badge of Courage

BRUCE DAWE
Selected Poems

WALTER DE LA MARE
Selected Poems

DANIEL DEFOE
A Journal of the Plague Year
Moll Flanders
Robinson Crusoe

CHARLES DICKENS
A Tale of Two Cities
Bleak House
David Copperfield
Dombey and Son
Great Expectations
Hard Times
Little Dorrit
Nicholas Nickleby
Oliver Twist
Our Mutual Friend
The Pickwick Papers

EMILY DICKINSON
Selected Poems

JOHN DONNE
Selected Poems

THEODORE DREISER
Sister Carrie

GEORGE ELIOT
Adam Bede
Middlemarch
Silas Marner
The Mill on the Floss

T. S. ELIOT
Four Quartets
Murder in the Cathedral
Selected Poems
The Cocktail Party
The Waste Land

J. G. FARRELL
The Siege of Krishnapur

GEORGE FARQUHAR
The Beaux Stratagem

WILLIAM FAULKNER
Absalom, Absalom!
As I Lay Dying
Go Down, Moses
The Sound and the Fury

HENRY FIELDING
Joseph Andrews
Tom Jones

F. SCOTT FITZGERALD
Tender is the Night
The Great Gatsby

E. M. FORSTER
A Passage to India
Howards End

ATHOL FUGARD
Selected Plays

JOHN GALSWORTHY
Strife

MRS GASKELL
North and South

WILLIAM GOLDING
Lord of the Flies
The Inheritors
The Spire

OLIVER GOLDSMITH
She Stoops to Conquer
The Vicar of Wakefield

ROBERT GRAVES
Goodbye to All That

GRAHAM GREENE
Brighton Rock
The Heart of the Matter
The Power and the Glory

THOMAS HARDY
Far from the Madding Crowd
Jude the Obscure
Selected Poems
Tess of the D'Urbervilles
The Mayor of Casterbridge
The Return of the Native
The Trumpet Major
The Woodlanders
Under the Greenwood Tree

L. P. HARTLEY
The Go-Between
The Shrimp and the Anemone

NATHANIEL HAWTHORNE
The Scarlet Letter

SEAMUS HEANEY
Selected Poems

JOSEPH HELLER
Catch-22

ERNEST HEMINGWAY
A Farewell to Arms
For Whom the Bell Tolls
The African Stories
The Old Man and the Sea

GEORGE HERBERT
Selected Poems

HERMANN HESSE
Steppenwolf

BARRY HINES
Kes

HOMER
The Iliad
The Odyssey

ANTHONY HOPE
The Prisoner of Zenda

GERARD MANLEY HOPKINS
Selected Poems

WILLIAM DEAN HOWELLS
The Rise of Silas Lapham

RICHARD HUGHES
A High Wind in Jamaica

THOMAS HUGHES
Tom Brown's Schooldays

ALDOUS HUXLEY
Brave New World

HENRIK IBSEN
A Doll's House
Ghosts
Hedda Gabler

HENRY JAMES
Daisy Miller
The Ambassadors
The Europeans
The Portrait of a Lady
The Turn of the Screw
Washington Square

SAMUEL JOHNSON
Rasselas

BEN JONSON
The Alchemist
Volpone

JAMES JOYCE
A Portrait of the Artist as a Young Man
Dubliners

JOHN KEATS
Selected Poems

RUDYARD KIPLING
Kim

D. H. LAWRENCE
Sons and Lovers
The Rainbow
Women in Love

CAMARA LAYE
L'Enfant Noir

HARPER LEE
To Kill a Mocking-Bird

LAURIE LEE
Cider with Rosie

THOMAS MANN
Tonio Kröger

CHRISTOPHER MARLOWE
Doctor Faustus
Edward II

ANDREW MARVELL
Selected Poems

W. SOMERSET MAUGHAM
Of Human Bondage
Selected Short Stories

GAVIN MAXWELL
Ring of Bright Water

J. MEADE FALKNER
Moonfleet

HERMAN MELVILLE
Billy Budd
Moby Dick

THOMAS MIDDLETON
Women Beware Women

THOMAS MIDDLETON *and* WILLIAM ROWLEY
The Changeling

ARTHUR MILLER
Death of a Salesman
The Crucible

JOHN MILTON
Paradise Lost I & II
Paradise Lost IV & IX
Selected Poems

V. S. NAIPAUL
A House for Mr Biswas

SEAN O'CASEY
Juno and the Paycock
The Shadow of a Gunman

GABRIEL OKARA
The Voice

EUGENE O'NEILL
Mourning Becomes Electra

GEORGE ORWELL
Animal Farm
Nineteen Eighty-four

JOHN OSBORNE
Look Back in Anger

WILFRED OWEN
Selected Poems

ALAN PATON
Cry, The Beloved Country

THOMAS LOVE PEACOCK
Nightmare Abbey and *Crotchet Castle*

HAROLD PINTER
The Birthday Party
The Caretaker

PLATO
The Republic

ALEXANDER POPE
Selected Poems

THOMAS PYNCHON
The Crying of Lot 49

SIR WALTER SCOTT
Ivanhoe
Quentin Durward
The Heart of Midlothian
Waverley

PETER SHAFFER
The Royal Hunt of the Sun

WILLIAM SHAKESPEARE
A Midsummer Night's Dream
Antony and Cleopatra
As You Like It
Coriolanus
Cymbeline
Hamlet
Henry IV Part I
Henry IV Part II
Henry V
Julius Caesar
King Lear
Love's Labour Lost
Macbeth
Measure for Measure
Much Ado About Nothing
Othello
Richard II
Richard III
Romeo and Juliet
Sonnets
The Merchant of Venice
The Taming of the Shrew
The Tempest
The Winter's Tale
Troilus and Cressida
Twelfth Night
The Two Gentlemen of Verona

GEORGE BERNARD SHAW
Androcles and the Lion
Arms and the Man
Caesar and Cleopatra
Candida
Major Barbara
Pygmalion
Saint Joan
The Devil's Disciple

MARY SHELLEY
Frankenstein

PERCY BYSSHE SHELLEY
Selected Poems

RICHARD BRINSLEY SHERIDAN
The School for Scandal
The Rivals

WOLE SOYINKA
The Lion and the Jewel
The Road
Three Shorts Plays

EDMUND SPENSER
The Faerie Queene (Book I)

JOHN STEINBECK
Of Mice and Men
The Grapes of Wrath
The Pearl

LAURENCE STERNE
A Sentimental Journey
Tristram Shandy

ROBERT LOUIS STEVENSON
Kidnapped
Treasure Island
Dr Jekyll and Mr Hyde

TOM STOPPARD
Professional Foul
Rosencrantz and Guildenstern are Dead

JONATHAN SWIFT
Gulliver's Travels

JOHN MILLINGTON SYNGE
The Playboy of the Western World

TENNYSON
Selected Poems

W. M. THACKERAY
Vanity Fair

DYLAN THOMAS
Under Milk Wood

EDWARD THOMAS
Selected Poems

FLORA THOMPSON
Lark Rise to Candleford

J. R. R. TOLKIEN
The Hobbit
The Lord of the Rings

CYRIL TOURNEUR
The Revenger's Tragedy

ANTHONY TROLLOPE
Barchester Towers

MARK TWAIN
Huckleberry Finn
Tom Sawyer

JOHN VANBRUGH
The Relapse

VIRGIL
The Aeneid

VOLTAIRE
Candide

EVELYN WAUGH
Decline and Fall
A Handful of Dust

JOHN WEBSTER
The Duchess of Malfi
The White Devil

H. G. WELLS
The History of Mr Polly
The Invisible Man
The War of the Worlds

ARNOLD WESKER
Chips with Everything
Roots

PATRICK WHITE
Voss

OSCAR WILDE
The Importance of Being Earnest

TENNESSEE WILLIAMS
The Glass Menagerie

VIRGINIA WOOLF
Mrs Dalloway
To the Lighthouse

WILLIAM WORDSWORTH
Selected Poems

WILLIAM WYCHERLEY
The Country Wife

W. B. YEATS
Selected Poems

York Handbooks: list of titles

YORK HANDBOOKS form a companion series to York Notes and are designed to meet the wider needs of students of English and related fields. Each volume is a compact study of a given subject area, written by an authority with experience in communicating the essential ideas to students of all levels.